IN CELEBRATION OF FORMULA 9

While spending extensive time abroad my friend Elizabeth announced that she was writing a book to help modern generations navigate life's challenges – which she saw as even more necessary in the present day. This idea was prompted by her encounters with many US, European, and Middle Eastern young adults looking for deeper meaning in their lives. In my ethnic, religious studies, and critical thinking courses at university, students were searching for answers and truths more so than the generations before them - something that would guide them to a heightened consciousness and to unravel the 'big' questions of life, such as what is the nature of existence? Who am I? Why am I here? What sense can be made of collective pain and suffering? And so on.

During our many catch-up sessions - some, intercontinental, Elizabeth would give me updates, and we discussed the book concepts and the ingenious name 'Formula 9'. The book was almost finished in a year, and I was privileged to have a draft copy. Wow!!! I was excited. I tested parts of the text material in real time with the young adults in my courses. The feedback and subsequent discussions from students was overwhelmingly thoughtful and positive. They were grateful to have someone discuss matters around 'being', purpose and life skills in terms they could relate to. Based on this response I designed an online interactive curriculum from Formula 9 for a global university textbook portal. This was for my hundreds of online students. And from this the evaluations and comments continued to be positive from groups who tend to be critical of almost everything authored by 'baby boomers'. That was a sure sign that the book was relevant and helpful to today's up and coming people who may be millennials, Generation Z and those generations that follow.

Dr. Taylor has developed an effective and down-to-earth resource to help modern generations meet the unique challenges in today's world of high-pitched social media, accelerating technology, changing values and economies, and moral contradictions. Not telling them what to think but providing 'keys' and a comprehensive toolbox to help them to better 'know' themselves, to affirmatively engage the world around them, find their place in it, and chart their futures. We have now been living with this work of her genius since 2016, and it has stood the test of time and scrutiny. Her work continues to inspire seekers in life's journey. Formula 9 is a book for the ages and in reality, it speaks to anyone. Enjoy!

Dr. Derrick Spiva, Businessman and Professor in Cultural/Religious Studies

FORMULA 9

Fortified Conscious Living for Modern Generations

2nd Edition

FORMULA 9

Fortified Conscious Living for Modern Generations

2nd Edition

Dr. Elizabeth D. Taylor

WISDOM TO GO, INC.

San Francisco, California

Phoenix, Arizona. USA

FORMULA 9

Fortified Conscious Living for Modern Generations

2nd Edition

Published by Wisdom to Go, Inc.

San Francisco, California

Phoenix, Arizona. USA

Dr. Elizabeth D. Taylor, Publisher

Yvonne Rose/Quality Press, Book Packager

Thiệu Quân Nguyễn, Cover Designer

Russell Leavitt, 'Formula 9 Keys' Graphic Design

Copyright © 2017 and 2022 by Dr. Elizabeth D. Taylor

Paperback ISBN #: 978-1-0880-4527-5

Hardcover ISBN #: 978-1-0880-6270-8

eBook ISBN #: 978-1-0880-7822-8

Library of Congress Control Number: 2022913083

DEDICATION

To Julian-Sebastian
and his loving family of friends.

Formula 9

ACKNOWLEDGEMENTS

I extend my appreciation to Dr. Derrick Spiva, for seeing and embracing the importance of this work and witnessing its journey to reach and touch lives.

Thank you, Dr. Paul Rosenthal for your enduring intrinsic support. My equal gratitude is for your seasoned input on some essentials of financial and money management.

And I am entirely grateful to all of the 'fortified' modern generation adults I encountered in Europe, the Middle East, and in the US who inspired and encouraged me in your own ways to generate this book.

CONTENTS

Contents

Formula 9

INTRODUCTION
ABOUT and HOW to
Read This Book

The purpose of spiritual growth and evolution is
to attain understanding of the necessity of doing good
and living in harmony with Cosmic Laws; and to express
your Divine Nature in everything you think, say and do.
- Sacred Rosicrucian Text

Life is the grand adventure. It is a gift. *Formula 9* is here to help you make the most of this experience. *Formula 9* is a 'tool-based' resource that enables you to fortify your consciousness to live better and master your life. It is grounded in practical and indigenous wisdoms, spiritual truths, and depth psychology. With *Formula 9* you can grow your understanding of the challenges and problems that come with everyday living in our world. With *Formula 9* you can develop life skills to realize your desires and goals. The information contained in this book is nothing new. It is ages old knowledge which has been culled, reformulated, and rendered for you, especially.

We are given a formidable tool to understand the meaning of our lives – that tool is 'consciousness'. Taking the degree and quality of our consciousness seriously is necessary and vital to navigate the world of today; this is becoming increasingly hard to ignore. We occupy a densely rational world where concepts of personal and spiritual growth and evolution are not valued, encouraged or mainstreamed; this is a world that over-externalizes people and crowds out introspection and the inner life. Consciousness-raising and mindful personal evolution are generally dismissed in the popular culture as inconsequential and without substance, as fluffy and weakening - not reflecting the pragmatism and hard sciences that predominate and generally define the way people 'should' live. However, this is changing as more people are gradually 'waking up' and becoming *"woke"*, as they say. Subsequently researchers and scholars are taking note that as a whole, young and next generation adults - what this author collectively calls: *'Modern generations'* or the 'new people', are open and want more alternative spiritual information and knowledge.

This book may introduce concepts which are foreign to the way you traditionally learned and understand the nature of our reality up to now. It may challenge your worldview, perceptions and belief systems. However, the knowledge here is potent and necessary for our times; it represents the more obscured 'facts of life'. And I suppose that somehow deep within yourself you *know* this. As you read and digest *Formula 9* these concepts will resonate at some level within your consciousness. *Formula 9* can help you to 'remember'. To make the most of *Formula 9* take its content easy and in small doses; make it a companion and guide for your reflections that you can grow with. Approach it with an open mind. Take your time and share *Formula 9* with others. It has a timeless message that is vital, relevant and can add leverage and volume to your life.

Due to the comprehensive nature of *Formula 9,* some redundancies are deliberate and necessary. As well, the language speaks alternately directly to you, the reader and makes references to second and third persons, all of which includes YOU. Respectfully.

In gratitude for this opportunity to present *Formula 9* to you.

Dr. Elizabeth Taylor

OVERVIEW

Modern Generations
- Strengths, Limitations,
Threats and Opportunities

The meaning of life is to be the eyes, ears and
the consciousness of the Creator of the universe.

- R.A.P Ferreira

Reality is where it's at. This pertains to the reality in the world, the reality in your dreams and desires and the reality of your living consciousness. There is nothing to escape from, but everything to go towards.

Welcome to *Formula 9*. This forward-looking 'tool-based' resource book is conceived and written exclusively with you in mind. *Formula 9* is a comprehensive combination of ingredients or *keys* that constitute expanding one's consciousness, which is essential to personal growth and evolution. You are the post baby boomer generations - and you are special. Demographers have observed and studied your generations profusely. In fact, you are the most studied generations of all time. And there is a reason for this. As a baby boomer, I am fascinated by you and excited about the world you have the potential to create; and are already doing so. You defy conventional mindsets, values and lifestyles that have preponderated and generated the world as we know it. From all the researching and 'head-scratching' around your values, tendencies, wiles and ways, the consensus is that you represent the refreshing and new promise the world duly needs.

And it is people like me who look upon you with respect, gladness, and anticipation of the wondrous things you will do to shape and revitalize life on this planet.

You are those who entered this world between the early 1980s to the early 2000s. You are the children and the grandchildren of the baby boomers. Your generations are inheriting a world that is gyrating with accelerating change and uncertainty, and which is impacting you more than the baby boomer generation. You are the emergent leaders - movers, shakers, and architects of a world in need of transforming. The world is your project and your laboratory for the experimentation of new ideas, concepts, and ways of knowing and being. If one were to do a SWOT analysis of your status in the world today, it might look something like this:

Strengths. Modern generation adults stand to be the most progressive in the history of humankind; the same rings true for the generations that follow them. You understand things instinctively. You are the 'indigos' - the new people on the block, poised to create a different world - one that moves towards peace, one that works in harmony with the earth, one with less suffering and one that generates human systems, which allows individuals to rise to their highest potentials.

Your generations are characterized by a fierce independence, proactivity, creativity, boldness and intellectual curiosity and genius, community, and communicating; you have made these into virtues. Your generations are 'at home' with diversity and differences. You can see the bigger picture of global connectedness. Your generations are socially and environmentally conscious with a progressive approach to economics and politics, equality and justice and even time-honored systems of religious faith. You want to do the right things. And you have the numbers as the largest generations in the history of the world. In some countries adults 35 years and under constitute 70% of the population. Modern generations around the world are a huge part of the voting block and are coming of age as powerful consumers and leaders. We can hope that during your generations the whole human race can be rendered conscious beyond hateful conflicts, shallowness and over-materialization, which is the goal of evolution.

Limitations. Modern generations specifically are disproportionately burdened with economic uncertainty. They are still mostly at the 2008 economic status levels with high debt and unemployment in a vacillating and competitive job market. They are plagued by uncertain financial futures and generally have economic lifestyles that are at a lower status than preceding generations. In a world that requires money in all things, this is a handicap that stifles the lives and freedoms of many. The distractions that abound in the lifestyles of modern generation adults are also a limitation. These distractions are fostered by the technologies that are entrenched in their lifestyles, and to a large degree, it stems from the social programming that focuses people outside of themselves to be more *externalized* rather than valuing the depths and richness of the inner life.

Threats. Your life is a sacred journey. The 'real' tools needed to navigate the world especially as it is today, are generally not taught in our main institutional 'learning' systems of schools and colleges, families, and religion. *Why is this?* Let's be candid. These socialization institutions instill values that steer us to adapt and conform to a prescribed world and psychological landscape. This is not a bad thing. It is how things work and what keeps society organized, manageable and to some degree predictable – given our collective capacities, resources and the state of the world. In this process people, by and large are rational consumers and workers, and I put it to you again: *Externalized* from their truest nature. And now in the 21st century - and as some would call it, the *"crazy world"*, up is down, right is left, and it is getting harder to distinguish good from bad. Time honored socialization institutions are coming up short to help you to understand yourself deeply and your inherent power to wield more control over your life experiences than you can imagine. These old systems do not provide you with the tools needed to navigate the world today which requires cognitive independence, new thinking and visions, alternate directions, and *spirituality - being focused and more concerned with the human spirit and soul over material things.*

The dynamism and rapidity of today's world requires heightened awareness and discernment. The raging distractions in the lifestyles of modern generations make the need for these qualities more acute. The modern generations' culture exhibits a marked familiarity and reliance on communications, social networks and media, and digital technologies. Proliferating technologies, and the ease with which they are accessed, generates perpetual distractions for modern generation adults along with the pull to adopt over-externalized and often, 'too busy' lifestyles. This becomes a self-fulfilling loop because adults 35 years and under were born into and grew up in the age of high-technology – and that is pretty much 'all they know', so to speak. Yet, technologies take up space and time that can otherwise be used to cultivate the awareness and higher consciousness, and life tools that are just as rapidly becoming so essential.

Opportunities. Collectively speaking, you are the solution, and there is more power in the solution than in the problems of this world. Not only are your generations more than others making life boosting decisions and choices, but yours have significant ramifications in the world as you are also prone to be visionaries and entrepreneurs. You are the generations to change the landscape and help shift humanity towards the 'light' of existence, making peace no longer just an ideal and making deep personal fulfillment a dominant quality that more people can aspire to and access.

With a 'fortified' consciousness, modern generations can change long-standing obstructions to the evolution of humankind. You do not need to regard old systems as standards of life for all people and for all time. You are the ones to re-write the script. This is the opportunity. The world is watching you - the world is in fact, reconfiguring itself to accommodate you and the new consciousness you represent.

Consciousness is everything. An expanded consciousness is priceless and more of a possibility today due to the many advances in human research, to social rethinking and openings, and to the emerging linkages among science, psychology, and spirituality. Unfettered discovering, cultivating, and extending a higher consciousness into the world is the opportunity that now meets you. When you have arrived at a radiant level of consciousness that sets you apart from who you were before; when you behold and wield its enormous power and witness what it manifests in your life on mental, emotional, spiritual, and experiential platforms, and how it spurs your

6

personal evolution, believe me, you will not trade *your* consciousness for all the riches, fame, and fortunes of the world.

Growing Consciousness

What does it mean to grow one's consciousness? The traditional definition of consciousness is: The state or quality of awareness, of being aware of an external object or something within oneself. Consciousness is the ability to feel, it is a 'wakefulness' as if from being asleep; it is having a sense of selfhood, and self-determination which is the execution of control over the system of the mind. The term 'consciousness' was earliest used in the 1500's and was derived from the word '*conscious*' which meant *together* and *to know*. The term was further used to mean '*knowing with oneself*'; '*sharing knowledge with oneself about something*'; or figuratively meaning '*knowing that one knows*' - turning one's eyes inward with intention and keeping them there for a spell.

Consciousness in our present-day context is to be awake and fully aware or to be decidedly on the path of wakefulness; AND it is acting on that awareness - basing your behavior and actions on the heightened awareness that you are gaining. You might ask, *"To be awake from what or aware of what?" "What does it mean to 'raise my consciousness', and why would I want to do this?"*

'Waking up in awareness', which is to honor and lift your consciousness, is not fundamentally a spiritual matter; it keeps you planted in spiritual and physical/material planes – not one over the other; doing so can enhance your spiritual development. Raising your consciousness is an essential life skill; it is the progressive mastery of your mind and emotions and therefore, your life. This means waking up from the slumber of 'ignorance' and 'blindness' to 'self'; it is a gradual process which includes:

1. Making thoughtful, intelligent, and discerning decisions and choices; and trusting the decisions and choices that you make - that come from you.

2. Cultivating and maintaining a healthy mental and emotional state of mind – being able to navigate the fluctuations and distractions of your mental and emotional states. Being cognizant of your thoughts and emotions, knowing their quality and content, when they arise, their sources and why they arise. Isolating and purging counterproductive beliefs and mental habits while developing and instilling productive ones.

3. Becoming intimately acquainted with your mental and emotional processes to the point where you can see how these directly translate into and color your experiences.

4. Separating mental constructs and feelings from what you perceive to be your identity; it is knowing that thoughts/feelings and identity are not the same things.

5. It is to improve upon whatever programming you've incurred and cultivating and operating from a realistic and effective model of reality – valuing both subjective and objective realities, becoming more of an independent critical thinker - questioning.

6. It is diving deeper and reaching higher to discover, uncover and express the best and highest parts of yourself, valuing personal growth and being a lifelong learner.

Raising consciousness traverses a lifetime. It is not finished in a day or during a weekend retreat. You gradually broaden your capacity to grow your consciousness over many years. It takes time, effort, discipline, and determination. And I cannot say enough that doing so is not a luxury, it is increasingly necessary to life on the planet today and tomorrow.

However, we are not educated in this way – to value this basic tenet of human growth – not in early childhood or college education, not in our family or religious institutions, and certainly not in the workplace. We are not generally taught to know ourselves and to reap our finest human qualities. We are not taught nor given the tools on how to make the most important decisions of our lives, nor how to know and nurture the attainment of our truest desires. Yet over a lifetime, this capacity will become more significant than anything you ever learned in school or at university. This is the case because this is what we are meant to do.

The good news is that you don't have to wait a lifetime to develop and apply the tools presented here to embark on the journey towards greater consciousness. And if this is not something you wish to do or are not ready to do at this time, you are welcome and supported to stop reading here.

Making the Choice

Consciousness is independent of the typical characteristics that we think totally defines who we are individually. It does not vary from country to country. Growing your consciousness takes you beyond the intellect, beyond race, gender, culture, class, and ethnicity. It takes you beyond family origins and ancestry. It even takes you beyond the parameters of your personality. At the same time, growing your consciousness does not forsake these things, but embraces, compliments and incorporates these to elevate you into a more total 'being'. It grounds your overall identity. It makes you MORE and brings you closer to who you are meant to be.

Consciousness cannot be measured as in intelligence, but in terms of how much 'light' a person reflects through their consciousness – in their 'beingness'. There are differing qualities of consciousness. While no one is born inferior to another, people reflect inferior and superior states of consciousness - operating on higher and lower levels of consciousness. Consciousness is the one human characteristic that makes people equal or unequal. The quality of consciousness that people manifest is in direct correlation to the choices they make to either evolve towards their higher selves or not. At some point in every life, one is faced with this choice. In this sense what intrinsically and apparently differentiates one person from another is the degree, intensity, and radiance of the 'light' they reflect through their consciousness.

The Formula 9 Keys for Living More Consciously

Formula 9 is a series of *'awarenesses'*, intentions and actions that in their sum enables you to attain the result of having an expanding and higher consciousness. These are organized and expressed in 9 Keys as listed below and thoroughly discussed in Book chapters 1-6, which are the 'formulaic' chapters. Book chapters 7, 8 and 9 supplement the formulaic ones and are relevant to the process of strengthening your awareness; these chapters round out the Formula 9.

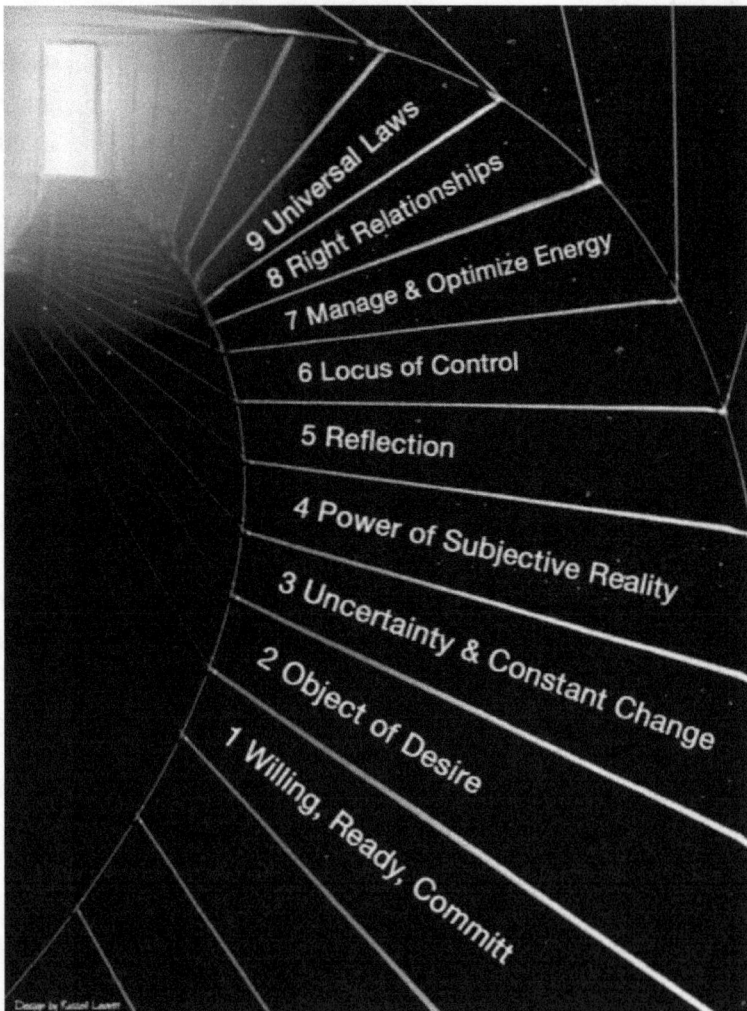

Key #1: Growing your consciousness begins with the intention to be *willing* to become and live a more conscious life; and *ready* and *commit* to this. *(Chapter 1)*

Key #2: Once you are willing, ready, and committed to growing your consciousness it is necessary to cultivate your awareness of your inherent *object of desire*. This is to know what thing(s) or experience(s) you desire above all, and that drives and motivates you. This is something that you believe will fulfill and satisfy you intrinsically at any given point in your life. *(Chapter 1)*

Key #3: Recognize and accept the perpetual state of *uncertainty and constant change* in the world that must be navigated to achieve the object of your desire; and develop your capacity to work with change. *(Chapter 1)*

Key #4: Develop the awareness, appreciation, and ability to access the *power of subjective reality* that coexists with and informs objective reality. *(Chapter 1)*

Key #5: Develop the capacity to *reflect* and build a ritual of reflection into your lifestyle. *(Chapter 2)*

Key #6: Become aware of your *locus of control* and exercise your 'free will' to shift or modify this orientation to include elements of internal and external loci of control orientations. *(Chapter 3)*

Key #7: Develop the capacity to manage and *optimize your energy and increase your vibration. (Chapter 4)*

Key #8: Attract, cultivate. and retain the *right relationships* for support and positive evolution. *(Chapter 5)*

Key # 9: Acknowledge and *work in harmony with universal laws* of mind and spirit. *(Chapter 6)*

This series of *awarenesses*, intentions and actions do not necessarily occur in sequence. However, this process must begin with the first Key, which is willingness, readiness, and a commitment to grow one's consciousness. Nothing can happen without this. From this point of incipient awareness, one can expand their consciousness through all Keys which can be done concurrently. Together, all 9 Keys represent a process that can produce enduring and fruitful outcomes.

Consciousness is layered. There are many realms of consciousness to be explored and reached. We humans utilize a very small percentage of our psyche during a lifetime; psyche being the totality of the human mind, consciousness, subconsciousness, and superconscious. Expanding your consciousness is a constant - it is a continuum, it occurs over a lifetime, and there is all the time in the world to do this. It is not something that you begin and end. Nor is it a goal. It is, however, a *way of life* and a means to your ongoing personal evolution and enhanced quality of life.

There is much to know, to see and do, to be discovered, to be rendered, renewed, and expressed in your personal journeys. You are at the timely evolutionary trajectory to meet this well.

I'm smiling at you.

Dr. Elizabeth

CHAPTER ONE

PURPOSE

Physical death I do not fear,
but death of consciousness I do fear.
- Anonymous

He (and she) who has a WHY to
live can bear almost any HOW.
- Nietzsche

The Purposeful Journey

Personal Growth and Personal Evolution

Personal growth and personal evolution are both important and compatible processes in the human experience. Personal growth is changing and improving aspects of yourself. This can be in relation to goals and developing the skills needed to have a certain quality of life. Personal growth is more associated with how to best function within mundane, objective, everyday reality. Personal evolution is about becoming the person you truly are meant to be - allowing yourself to unfold to express the loftier qualities of your character as fully as possible. This means going deeper into your depths and surfacing who you are at a spirit/soul level, and you do this within the context of the universal principles that govern yours and everyone's existence. Personal evolution is a much more radical process than personal growth, and which is often met with extreme tests and challenges. Personal evolution is about developing one's highest capacities and higher consciousness; and applying these in all that one does. The purpose for every human is to evolve; becoming more conscious is the purposeful goal. Through personal growth we develop the *tools* and *'awarenesses'* that help us evolve and become more conscious.

Eckhart Tolle stated that *"Life will give you whatever experience is most helpful for the evolution of your consciousness."* Our time on earth is not merely a span of life – with us taking up space; it is truly an odyssey - a time-intensive, manifold process for development, betterment, and evolution; there is no way to halt the process without ending it. Evolving is innate and required of every one of us whether we acknowledge this or not. Inevitable growth and evolution without the 'right' awareness and cultivation can be lopsided and distorted. Each person on the planet has an intrinsic responsibility for his and her own life; as well, we have the privilege to pursue our noble desires. And that which we desire and achieve are indelibly tied to our personal evolutions.

The Pursuit of Happiness

The earthly experience allows us to manifest and fulfill what yearns to be expressed deep within us and to evolve. At the same time, we are beings of desire - driven to satisfy an impulse that would make us happy, which is unique to each person. We are born with a 'desire' gene. Desire is in our DNA. It is the impetus within us to fulfill a 'wish' or an 'inclination' in our lived experiences. This desire becomes increasingly apparent and clear over a lifetime. With growth, experience, and personal knowledge this 'desire' changes and morphs, but it is always a steady *reaching* for something that propels and motivates us in one way or another.

What people desire most of all are qualities – not things or situations. Although the desire may seem to be a thing or situation, in truth it is the quality and 'raised state of being' that it brings that satisfies our desires. It is the attainment of these qualities that brings about the experience of happiness. These qualities can be peace of mind and relief from anxiety and fear; these can be the want of financial security, contentment, love, wisdom, freedom, good health, personal accomplishment and fulfillment, or to create and contribute to the social welfare. There is no activity in this life that is not driven by an inner urge that yearns to fulfill these kinds of qualities, which cannot be seen, touched, nor experienced with our senses; they cannot be handled, weighed, or measured. Again, the desire for these qualities, ergo the need for the happiness they bring is encoded in our DNA. This is the natural state of being human.

The *pursuit of happiness* is not merely something that is written into our constitution. The desire for happiness is indelibly ingrained in us as individuals and collectively it unifies us as sentient beings. It is a birthright – a seed within our consciousness that is longing always to be fulfilled in some manner. A teacher may desire to help others to learn; a policeman may desire to protect; a father or mother may desire to love and care for their children; a bachelor, to generate and belong to a family; a writer may desire creative expression and recognition, while a politician may desire power – all of which translate to a 'happiness' – a quality in their lives and a raised sense of being. Desires are neither inherently good nor bad, and are different and relevant for each person, as well as the way a person pursues those desires – which shapes the decisions and choices one makes and sets the direction and tone of their lives. The drive to satisfy a desire and to evolve are two fundamental aspects of our existences which defines and gives momentum and purpose to our lives.

Joined with the impetus to satisfy the desire encoded in our DNA is the universal *imperative* to evolve to our highest potential and to increase our capacity to reflect and receive *light*. We are far more aware and deliberate in our pursuit to satisfy our innate desires than we are of the evolutionary process that is also a part of our sojourn on earth. In fact, this is something that is taken for granted with our awareness of the need for personal evolvement being more on a subconscious level. Pursuit of desire for 'happiness' becomes more active, whereas evolving is passive and usually by happenstance. Growing your consciousness is to become aware that these two processes are an indelible part of your human experience. These are happening simultaneously and within the framework of universal principles.

The Heart of Desire

The impulse to reach for and achieve a desire is independent of the actual desire. For instance, it is not always the case that the desire we reach for supplements our need for growth, evolution, and fulfillment. Often people are steered far from their truest potential and satisfaction in life by false desires.

There are countless stories from individual's lives that illustrate this paradox of human existence. For example: *Take the man of wealth who has all the money he could ever want to buy and possess without limits. But the real object of his desire was not the wealth - or so he thought at the beginning. He may rather have wanted to be an artist and create something - to produce a masterpiece from his own genius. And while he pursued and achieved his wealth there was always something nagging within him - some point of self-deficiency, that could not be identified or known. He became depressed in his wealth because all of his money could not bring him 'himself' and who he was truly meant to be. Or take the young women born on the poor side of the tracks. She was told time and time again that she needed to get an education if she was to rise above her status and be successful in life. She was also made to believe that she should marry, have children, and get a good job and have good friends. She believed that would be the key to a happy life and followed that path. She worked hard, saved, grew in her position at her firm. She too, had the disquieting inner nagging feeling of incompleteness within her after she pursued what she thought would make her happy. She was not fulfilled in her life, yet she continued to work herself to the bone to avoid dealing with the anguish in her psyche. In these instances, the individuals aimed for a desire with little connection to 'themselves' nor heeded the promptings of their inner life. They did what they were advised and taught to do to be accomplished people - they listened to the louder voices that spoke to them. But in their reach for something they never got to know who they really were and their truest values and aspirations. Both represent textbook examples of externalized lives - whether by choice or default. The result is the same. And the world is full of half and falsely lived lives.*

Facing this scenario, you might ask yourself if you are *ready* and *willing* to step forward and *commit* to be a 'conscious participant' in your personal evolution - to be the best that you can be and achieving what is important to make the most of your life experience. This is simply opening your eyes and thinking, intending, and affirming, *"Yes, I will be a full conscious participant in my unfolding life process."* The process will happen without your conscious participation, but stepping into this fully aware, ready, willing, and committing makes a difference - one as distinct as night and day. Expanding your consciousness deepens self-knowledge which helps you to discern the desires that compliment your evolutionary needs and fulfillment, and it can provide a clearing for you to see and reach for the *heart of your desire.*

The Object of Your Desire

There are deeper levels to desire related to concepts of God, divinity, or spiritual engrossment. The focus within these pages is on how desires per se, are the drivers for determining the quality of our everyday lives. Desire is what 'wills' you; desire is what sustains you. It is important to understand this AND to become intimately acquainted with what it is that you desire, because desire is so powerful! And humans will always be driven by a desire for something, be it companionship, security, things, honor, respect, fame, power, for peace or to create. There are many desires - and in each life there is one or more that dominates and pulls.

As creatures of desire our individual lives drives us to reach for an *'object of our desire'* amidst a raging sea of constant change, complexity, uncertainty, and our self-imposed limitations. Here, desire and control are compelling, and we strive for both to some degree. Control is both an 'end' and a 'means' in the fulfillment of 'desire'. Having our desires fulfilled gives us a sense of control over our reality and increases our sense of well-being. And in the pursuit of our desires, we are often also trying to exercise 'control'; this could be control over our environment, other people, or events. What obstructs and interferes with our plans to fulfill our desires is the heightened change, uncertainty, and complexity in the world, and which is becoming more dynamic - making it more challenging than ever for the average person to experience the satisfaction of truly achieving the object of his and her desire.

The Divine Laughter and the Illusion of Control

There is an adage that says: *"If you want to hear God laugh, then tell God your plans."* Whatever your concept of God may be, be it a higher power, intelligence, or Divine will, this notion applies. For me, I've heard the disembodied Divine laughter countless times in my journey, and precisely when I thought I had things all figured out.

Everything in this life is in the perpetual process of becoming and changing. Nothing really stays the same, not routines, schedules, plans, agreements, conditions, comforts, places or people, the world, etc. Our bodies even change without our consent. And time is an instigator. Everything is being born, growing, and dying and being refashioned and reborn into some other form or scene. In the very instance that something reaches its apex, it begins its decline. There is no reality that is fixed, and enduring – nothing is permanent but *change*. Things get better with change or not - always requiring the making of adjustments. Change with the need to adapt comes on the wings of the plans that we have and make for ourselves, and in our professional and work activities, which consumes a large portion of our lives.

Working to earn a living is a part of most adults' lives, and this is where change is most dramatic and significant as adult lives are so tied to work. Here, change is occurring at a faster pace in the world of work than it was 5 years ago, and 5 years ago it was faster than it was 10 years prior. In fact, change seems to be accelerating. Plans in the business world must have built in strategies to continually adapt to change. This is necessary more than ever before. Today's business trend has it that: Adhering to a firm and rigid plan is high risk and is a plan to fail; loopholes must be built into any blueprint to allow and accommodate inevitable shifts and deviations; and the timetable for any strategic plan must be fluid and flexible – able to bend and be redirected as the long-established standard 5-year timeframe for a business strategic plan is now obsolete. Within the past decade the traditional business strategic plan changed to 2 years; and it is now advantageous to plan within a 6 to 12-month window - sometimes even less. An emergent trend is for businesses to plan organically, which is to 'flow' with the dictates of change and adapt as needed – to be nimble. The rate and pace of change and complexity that are occurring at the macro level of business unerringly impacts and influences the micro level of a 'personal life' despite how people may plan and set goals in pursuit of their desires. Being employed for a lifetime with a company was a norm 15-20 years ago. That tradition is now a memory relegated to the generations of your parents and grandparents. Working to receive a pension is history for the most part. There is no security, there are no guarantees in employment today - not even for the highest performers as businesses collapse, merge and downsize and become increasingly competitive. Robots are replacing jobs as services are becoming automated in banks, medical offices, even in fast food restaurants. Technology drives much of the fast rate of change; we are in fact, forced into it in order to access needed services and to just get everyday things done, such as banking and arranging for medical care. The proliferation of innovations and ideas are diversifying our way of life – making it so that we cannot really thrive unless we are in the flow, constantly updating, and changing with change. With change comes uncertainty, and these in fact, are sisters.

It is only natural and instinctive that the dynamic and perpetual level of change and uncertainty in today's business and world landscapes compels us to seek some means of control to have confidence in our futures. The irony is that this is not achievable. This is an illusion and something we must learn to accept and manage. And guess what?! When it is all said and done at the office or work desk and you seek the comfort and sanctity of familiar relationships, you may also find that you cannot control people and those very close to you. No worries! We'll get to that later. It is a brave new world indeed!

Control is Partnering with Change

Change is not the enemy. Orienting one's mindset to regard change as a friend and a partner in one's personal journey is the best course. This gives you leverage. Fact is, in relation to change, what you really have is control over your perceptions, reactions and behaviors which grants you influence over circumstances. And that is a good thing. Additionally, change can help one learn, grow, and evolve if one allows this. Trusting, partnering and being proactive with change means developing the reflexes to adapt rather than resisting change whether it involves work and professional life, technology, circumstances, or people. Avoiding, fighting against or trying to control change places one in a perpetual state of unhappiness, like swimming upstream against strong currents of water. Recognizing that most times in today's world one must take things as they are, rather than pushing against and trying to control; this keeps one sane and balanced. Working with change means becoming an 'agent of change' to the degree that you can. This means getting out of your comfort zone when change calls you out instead of resisting it - seeing the possibilities it brings rather than the upsets and difficulties. Working proactively is becoming at ease with ambiguity. It is trusting change and letting change assist and benefit you. Assuming this kind of posture to be in a positive relationship with change reduces fear and any hold it may have on you.

While one is developing a positive and proactive relationship with change one must recognize that not all change is good and beneficial. There are changes for the better and changes for the worse, as it is said: '*Like going from the frying pan into the fire*'. This is where discernment, reflection, and the self-knowledge that one gains from these processes will serve and help you understand the forces at work with inevitable changes. The more you grow your consciousness, the better you can *see* and *know*, because you are working from a higher purview - like using peripheral vision to see the wider landscape rather than looking through a peephole. When you grow self-knowledge, you will know in your own time when and how to set a new course, make a move, or do something entirely different with your life, regardless of external factors. You can better anticipate change and plan for it.

So, as we desire and are moved to control our reality to achieve our desires, we must embrace change, uncertainty and complexity and welcome the Divine laughter! The confidence we seek for a secure future and access to achieve the object of our desire must come from new places now. In time, you may find yourself laughing too.

The Rule of Subjective Reality

Life is not just about having successes on the physical plane via amassing wealth, recognition, romance, possessions, or welding power. Life is not all about the material and mundane alone, it is not about what emanates exclusively from the objective reality in which the human kingdom tends to focus. We are born into and oriented towards physical/material reality, which is essentially, a reflection of a subtle subjective reality. Physical reality and lived experiences spring forth from the subjective reality - always. While we are not generally aware of this, we are compelled to know and understand this if we are to live the lives we want and desire.

The Objective and Subjective Realities

The parallel existence and difference between subjective reality (invisible) and objective reality or 'world of form' was recognized by the venerated philosopher, Plato. Our lives run on both objective and subjective tracks. Objective and subjective realities are always operating beyond our choices and free will. We have an inner reality and an outer reality, which are independent and at the same time co-dependent. In truth, we are always living betwixt and between these two realities, with the subjective reality being the 'orchestrater' and 'director' of most of our lived experiences.

Every day, every week, every month, and year, we, either consciously or not, are tasked to navigate objective and subjective realities to achieve the object of our desires and simply to go about our everyday lives. Objective reality consists of the 'things' and 'situations' that we are sure to exist independently of ourselves, and that can be verified through our senses and our ego personality consciousness, such as: The apparent world of objects; our sensations of touch, feeling, seeing, hearing, smelling; of possessions and observing and participating in the lived experiences of ourselves and of others. Basically, objective reality can be objectified. Subjective reality is essentially, that part of our experience that seemingly cannot be objectified or known through our senses. The truest distinctions between objective and subjective realities are vague - the lines do become blurred. For the sake of this discussion, let us understand subjective reality as the realm of thoughts, emotions, assumptions, intentions, instinct, intuition, hunches, shadow, insights, revelations, gut feelings, and so on - the subtle hits and impressions that cannot be readily objectified through our senses or ego personality state, but require focus, and a higher level of perception and psyche to comprehend. This is the world we trove when we reflect. The subjective reality is the pathway to the spiritual life, which is to be less guided by the ego and more by the impulses of the soul and spirit. Both objective and subjective realities are sources of information that we need to navigate this world of constant change, complexity, and uncertainty. Where objective reality is pretty much in your face, subjective reality requires attention, presence, and careful listening – tuning in. It is required and unavoidable in life's journey to navigate the objective and subjective realities, which are complimentary. Whether this is done willfully, or not, is a matter of personal choice; however, it behooves us to be conscious of this act as a part of deepening one's spiritual nature.

Control is Tuning in to Your Subjective Reality

The purposeful journey comes with some basic ABC's: *A* – You are born into *desire* and predisposed to satisfy a desire in an *apparent* objective reality/world; *B* - To effectively navigate the *apparent* reality to achieve the object of your desire, you must understand and navigate the subjective realms of reality. This is because subjective reality informs and to a large degree controls the objective or apparent reality, not vice versa. This makes the subjective reality far more vigorous. In fact, this is where the real action is!

There is a *truism* about subjective reality that we are compelled to know in order to achieve the 'objects of our desires'*: Important information is there.* Specifically, *our 'objective reality' is informed and shaped in the* *valley of our thoughts, emotions, and other elements of the subjective reality, which are tapped into profound universal forces. These universal forces or laws govern every life process, whether we choose to embrace this awareness or not.* This 'hidden' truism is not a part of our social education and learning or based on what we call 'knowledge'. Therefore, in *C* - We must understand that we are the co-authors of our objective and subjective realities. We are individually and collectively co-creating these realities in partnership with universal forces that operate with authority in our lives. And it is only through the combined channels of subjective and objective realities that we come to know the true 'object of our desire'.

I say again, the subjective world rules the objective world. The objective world springs from the subjective world of our thoughts, emotions, visions, and dreams. This is a mystical truth and an area where science is beginning to recognize and appreciate - that all objective experiences are generated from the realms of the subjective world. What precedes much of what we experience is a *thought.* This is truly without a doubt, the level at which we do have full control. At this level, control is increasing one's awareness of what is going on in the subjective realms of thought and emotion. One exhibits 'control' by trusting, navigating and maintaining a healthy climate in the subjective world of his and her thoughts and emotions.

The wealthy man and hard-working woman might have led different lives if the paths they chose were also informed by their subjective realities. Objective life has a loud voice. It dominates. It is brimming with activity and motion. It requires your full body and attention, and usually all the time. But living a life dominated by objective reality deprives you of the riches that lie waiting for you in the subjective realms. It makes your life shallow, superficial, and of little substance. You are not living in your fullness or assessing the greater parts of you and your capacity, which enriches and rounds out your lived experiences. Yet, the objective world is compelling, it pulls at you and is hard to resist - getting harder to resist in today's teaming and distracting world. It takes effort to negotiate a balance between the objective and subjective aspects of your life. And you need to have your feet planted in both realities. You can choose to have

23

this balance and dance between the subjective and objective realties. This helps you to have a stronger ability to manage change, uncertainty and complexity, bringing you closer to the truest object of your desire. This is a potent exercise in higher consciousness and a commanding life skill.

TOOLBOX

1. *Know What Desires Drive You.*

   Reflect to discover and acknowledge what you desire most. Then reflect on how this or these desires are guiding your decisions and choices; and how your desire(s) fit with your personal evolutionary process.

2. *Assess Your Relationship with Change.*

   Take a moment to reflect on past or present situations when change 'came knocking at your door' or when change just 'took over'. Do a review on how you met change, and generally, how are you doing on that front? This may be useful to know. Just being aware may inspire and enable you to make the right shifts where necessary.

3. *Take an Excursion into Your Subjective Realms.*

   Take a moment to visit with your subjective reality – you do this already every night when you sleep. Conduct a waking review of past hunches, insights, intuitions you've had, even your dreams – how did you view them, what did you do with them? Did you have any at all? Of course you did – try hard to recall. Then do the same review of your thoughts and emotions – just pull out a few and hold these up in the full view of your consciousness. What do these tell you? How do you feel about these? Do this exercise often to become better aware and acquainted with the subjective reality that surrounds and emanates through you. Go as deep as you can, and deeper still.

CHAPTER TWO

THE ALCHEMY OF REFLECTION

By all means take some time to be alone.
Salute thyself – see what thy soul doth wear
- Dare to look in thy chest; for 'tis thine own.
- George Herbert

When you see me sitting quietly like a sack left
behind on a shelf, don't think I need your chattering.
I'm listening to myself.
- Maya Angelou

Know Thyself!

Know thyself! This notion is expressed in every religious and spiritual text. It is a clarion call to all and throughout human existence. To know oneself is a first step towards personal power and mastery. *It is fundamentally: Knowledge of self and more so, understanding of self.* The work of 'self-knowing' can be laborious, but glorious; it is our most sacred imperative and key to real happiness. To defray from this privilege leaves one ignorant of the forces within them and inept at applying those forces.

Despite how well-educated or learned a person may be, the one area of knowledge that many and most people lack is that of 'self' in a culture, society and world that socializes us to focus outside of ourselves – to externalize our awareness, away from who we are.

To reflect is to know. Reflection brings your life into closer view; it makes sense of your life, and makes you more present with it. The act of reflection is a bending or folding back upon oneself. It is an inward glance. Self-reflection always yields something back. As in a mirror, *reflection* is the return of light back from a source. It is through the ritual of reflection that we come to know ourselves; and through which we access our higher selves and intuition for information and guidance amid the vagaries of ignorance, fear and 'false facts'. Once you are clear, willing, and ready to evolve your consciousness, reflection becomes the door that opens to you for compelling self-knowledge.

A lot of time, money and effort is spent on educating ourselves and developing skills and intellectual prowess. However, comparatively, we know little and less about ourselves. Without some degree of self-knowledge, a person is one-dimensional, leading a poorly directed and reactive life. The lack of personal knowledge makes a person vulnerable to manipulation - shuffled about as if a pawn on the chessboard of life – playing the game according to someone else's rules and designs. The tragedy of our times is that most people are unaware that they are so unaware.

A popular and useful adage states that *"There are three kinds of power: Money, Beauty and Knowledge."* This is true. Pragmatically speaking, self-knowledge is just as valid a form of power as is money and beauty. It is essential to living a more conscious life. Reflection enables you to find that quiet place inside where you can listen and hear what your heart is saying. When people are self-aware, they are truly empowered! And the way to get *there* begins with taking time to be alone within yourself – to be 'in' yourself.

Again, the journey of self-knowing is not something we are taught, nor is it valued in our culture and world. As a result, the desire to develop self-knowledge requires added effort to get past the countless distractions, distortions, and misinformation on our paths. The world culture and global mindset are ruled by a skewed Newtonian rationalism which increasingly exalts materialism, extroversion and shallowness over consciousness, inner-reality, and self-reflection. This is a tricky climate to try to stretch out and grow in for modern generations who are perpetually lured by digitized amusements and social delusions, and manipulative media and entertainment which are void of intellectual and spiritual nutritional value. The societal psyche is crammed 24/7 with 'junk food'. Where self-discovery and mastery might be encouraged, there is a preponderance of advertising, dizzying trends, rapacious infotainment, and the pull of over-externalizing. The fact is that one cannot afford *not* to be self-aware and self-possessed in our accelerated dynamic world today – a world that has people alienated and turning away from themselves - a culture that reminds you a hundred times a day that there are more interesting things to see and to know outside of *you*. A questioning and perhaps a willing and ready person like you must make a concerted effort to get a handle on *you* these days. In this ripe day and age, there are still many forces pulling against your becoming more self-aware. Knowing this gives you leverage as you step into self-knowledge and towards personal sovereignty.

A Little Pop Psychology

Popular psychology, sometimes referred to as 'pop psychology' provides some insights on self-knowledge as a fruitful by-product of reflection. 'Pop psychology' is a *'popularized'* body of psychologically-based concepts and theories about the human psyche and behavior - and which have credence. We accept what popular psychology espouses as true and effective because it has been tested and proven. Following are a few enduring psychological/behavioral models that provide clear windows to better understanding ourselves, our motivations, and drives.

Maslow's *'Hierarchy of Needs'* is a long-standing and reliable model for understanding human motivations. Dr. Abraham Maslow hypothesized, and it has been consistently validated that people's motivations operate on a hierarchy of needs - expressed in a pyramid scale with five ascending needs that people reach for as the needs below are satisfied. These needs from bottom to top are:

1. Biological or physiological needs, such as food, water, rest and shelter.

2. Safety and security needs, such as order, laws, and freedom from fear.

3. The need for relationships, intimacy, acceptance and belonging.

4. Self-esteem needs - to feel good about oneself through status, achievement, recognition and respect, and personal validation.

5. The need for self-actualization - to fulfill one's highest potential, deep personal growth or peak experiences.

MASLOW'S HIERARCHY OF NEEDS

According to Maslow, a person's needs must be satisfied at the lower levels before he or she progresses to higher, more complex levels of needs. Behavioralists observe that while most people achieve the needs at the lower levels of the hierarchy, fewer rise the scale beyond the third need which is for 'relationships and belongingness'; and even fewer rise the scale to achieve the fifth need for *'self-actualisation'* or actualization. This fifth level of 'self-actualization' is equated with higher personal evolution.

What makes this hierarchy of needs pertinent is that it corresponds to the impetus to both achieve desires and the imperative for personal evolution. Personal evolution or as Maslow would call it, *"self-actualisation"* is out of reach for most people, and for these reasons: The dense, rational, and over-externalized world people inhabit pressures and weighs them down - keeping them at the lower levels on the 'needs' scale; self-actualization is not generally promoted in our culture; and because the awareness and tools on how to achieve this level are not taught or generally available.

The *'Johari Window'* was made popular during the early 19th century and has withstood the test of time. It is simple and elegant. The Johari Window (created by psychologists Joseph Luft and Harrington Ingham) is a technique used to help people better understand their relationships with themselves and others. The 'window' is represented in four quadrants. Each quadrant represents an area of the psyche and its level of exposure to others and to the individual. For example, in the diagram below: Quadrant 1 represents the public self – suitably called the ARENA, it is the part known to the individual and to others. Quadrant 2 is the BLIND SPOT – part of the psyche that others generally see but what the individual does not see. However, it is a blind spot which peeks through in one's conscious awareness and experiences. The BLINDSPOT, when one is aware of it, allows one to identify and improve those parts of themselves that they may not like, that gets them into trouble, or that cause disturbances in their relationships with others. In Quadrant 3 there is the part of the self that is known only to the individual and not to others – usually by choice and is sometimes the 'self' that is play-acting at life. It is the FAÇADE. And there is Quadrant 4 which is the UNKNOWN part of the psyche that the individual nor others see. It contains subconscious information such as early childhood memories, undiscovered talents, and hidden personality traits, urges and drives.

THE JOHARI WINDOW

	Known to self	Not known to self
Known to others	**1.** THE ARENA	**2.** BLIND SPOT
Not known to others	**3.** FAÇADE	**4.** UNKNOWN

The 'Johari Window' helps us to understand just how much of ourselves we really know and what we do not know. The 'Johari Window' indicates that people generally know one half of who they are through the Arena and Façade; for the most part the Blind Spot and Unknown area represent the half of what people don't know about themselves. That half is a very important part of who we. Ironically, the Unknown aspect is the part of 'self' that should be known as much if not more than the other three; it is our 'shadow' and is highly operative in our waking and subjective lives. This is where reflection can help you to better know and appreciate the parts of you that you already know and to access the other half of YOU that you may not!

The fact that there are greater parts of ourselves that are unknown to us relates to another of my favorite tenets of 'pop psychology' from Neale Donald Walsch. It goes:

There are those who don't know, and don't know that they don't know. They are totally innocent, and it is for us to encourage them. Then there are those who don't know and know that they don't know. They are willing to know – teach them. Then there are those who don't know, but they think that they know. These are dangerous – avoid them. Then there are those who know, but then don't know that they know. They are asleep – Wake them. And there are those who know and know that they know. But do not follow them. Because they know that they know, they would not have you follow them. So, listen to what they have to tell you. Because they might say something that reminds you of what you already know.

The 'know' in this theorem refers to self-knowledge and wisdom. What is important to note here is that people indeed, have different qualities and capacities of 'self-knowing'. And people cannot move and develop beyond their capacities until they are aware and ready. The goal is to 'Know that You Know' - which involves knowing about YOU. This is where there is strength and personal power.

A third popular model for self-knowing is the Myers-Briggs Personality Type Indicator (MBTI). I used this model religiously in my teaching and consulting practices. Psychologist, Carl Jung was the father of 'typology' from which the Myers-Briggs testing instrument was derived. This is a schematic which outlines eight basic cognitive functions of the human personality as such:

INTROVERSION vs EXTROVERSION
INTUITIVE vs SENSING
THINKING vs FEELING
JUDGMENT vs PERCEPTIVE

In different configurations these compose 16 personality types among humans. Upon taking the MBTI test one can discover aspects of their personality that pertain to how they are energized, how they communicate and relate to others, and how they process information and make decisions and choices. This is one of the most reliable and eye-opening tools for developing self-knowledge, as well as better understanding others.

Finally, we hear a lot about 'positive thinking' in popular psychology. But 'positive thinking' is not the cure-all for our times when it comes to self-knowledge. Too much 'positive thinking' or 'positive thinking' at all costs is hype and has its traps. Positive thinking can be more helpful when it is grounded in a foundation of self-knowledge or a commitment to growing your knowledge of self. Positive thinking is most useful and impactful when it is balanced by a realistic assessment of a person's life, issues and situations, aspirations, and desires. Without this balance, positive thinking is delusional thinking and counterproductive window dressing. Reflection helps to avoid the traps and foibles of overindulging in positive thinking which can be comparable to the folly of Don Quixote battling windmills - delusional in his confidence that he will collect their spoils in his triumph. When you look at something square-on you can see it for what it is and then you can better accept it. Balance and personal stability come through self-awareness, from which comes self-acceptance. This is strengthening, it is healing. It is self-loving.

These popular models and other prevailing and established tenets of psychology are important and worth further study that will help foster personal understanding and compliment the concepts and tools provided in Formula 9. Reflection is an invaluable tool that helps one to discover his and her level of self-knowledge and to stretch their capacity to better 'know' themselves. These models are 'guides' that you can take into your reflections.

The What, Why, and How of Reflection

What is Reflection?

Again, our culture is not a reflective one. To self-reflect is not generally taught in our educational systems, nor is it the way we are prepared to meet and live and function in the world. We are socialized to externalize our lived experiences and to see that focus as having primary importance over the inner life, and to be our exclusive *raison d' etre*. We are in a culture that measures in terms of what we can objectify through our senses - to see, touch, hear, taste, smell or observe. The externalized experience is measurable. It is manageable. Within it we are taught strategies to navigate the world, to get a job, to formulate relationships, to plan to achieve a goal. We are externalized in all that we do. In our culture the real things to value and pursue in life are all outside ourselves. Reflection is foreign, strange, even ridiculed. We don't take seriously the shaman, the mystic, the seer. The quiet, introspective personality is usually the subject of bullying, and gets marginalized. Extroversion is valued, encouraged and rewarded; whereas introversion is misunderstood, undervalued, discouraged, and sometimes shamed.

You don't always need to be doing something. It's okay to slow down, to be still, to be idle and sit with yourself for a moment, an hour, a day, or longer. The Dutch have this tradition which is called: *niksen* - the art of purposely doing nothing. In *niksen*, one declutters the mind, and relieves stress and anxiety to boost creativity. This practice is a close cousin of reflection. In reflection, one pauses, but also to review, examine and become an observer of their internal and external life processes. In essence, one is *'processing the process'*. Despite how we are socialized, reflection is a natural human need, like food and love. It is a gateway and an inlet to personal knowledge and freedom, granting access and connection to one's subjective life that is rich, insightful and compelling. It is also an anecdote that supports positive mental and physical health by clearing out the junk, the cobwebs and the clutter of information, data, impressions, and experiences, etc. that our psyches accumulate – like a computer that needs debugging and clearing out every now and then. Reflection is a stress reducer, bringing 'relief' to the psyche - granting mental release and balance; it is a problem-solving tool, and aids in making decisions and setting goals. Reflection is a mediator in relationships as it helps you to better know, understand and define yourself in order to relate better to others.

There is indeed, an 'alchemy' involved in the personal reflection process. Alchemy was the ancient practice concerned with turning base metals into gold - literally. It was regarded as a magical process of transmutation, creation, and renewal. As in ancient alchemy, reflection is a catalyst and a trigger to transmute and transform lower states into higher states of consciousness – your gold! It ignites consciousness, making room for shifts in perspectives, habits, and approaches to the 'lived' experience for the better. It brings things into view and gets them unstuck as one meanders through their mind and the wide ocean of accumulated thoughts, insights, and impressions. Reflection is a doorway to access reservoirs of awareness that you need for your life. It prompts you to recall and remember. It sharpens your mental muscles and paves the way to commune with your higher self and higher wisdom - giving you access to the source from which your reality flows. It is a mechanism that energizes, nourishes, and can transform a life.

It is said that most of the world's problems would be solved if people took the time to reflect. This is because all of our lived experiences flow from inner states of consciousness, and reflection cultivates a refined and heightened state of consciousness. An unreflective life is an under-nourished and unbalanced life. We all have the capacity to reflect to different degrees. Reflecting can be a habit, even positively addictive and necessary once it is embraced and practiced regularly.

Why Reflect?

Like the universe, the capacity of the human psyche is vast! Yet, we typically use a miniscule part of this capacity. This is a scientific fact. However, we are endowed with the ability to access a 'personal reality' far beyond what we can imagine in our externalized lives. The grandeur of the physical universe is reflected within us, as we are indeed, composed of 'star stuff'. Reflection is the access point to the larger parts of ourselves. To 'reflect' is something we NEED to do in order to do the necessary 'processing' of everything and anything to do with our lives in the same way that our bodies naturally and must process food and nutrients.

Your life is a journey towards 'being' and 'becoming' a more conscious and evolved person to realize your fullest capacity as a human being on earth and as an evolving soul in spirit. The journey is not just all about doing and busying yourself with relentless activity. This is a distraction. The introspective journey prods you to have a balance between 'being' and 'doing'. Knowing yourself through reflection brings you closer to yourself, and to your personal power and the things that you desire and want to attract to you.

The steps we take across the rooms of our lives can be uncertain; the steps we take forward with an open mind must lead to that perfect of destinations – the truth of ourselves. Your mind is like a maze that requires careful conscious navigation and reflection. Reflection with an open mind allows you to sift through the information and 'trappings' that are there, to examine your assumptions, redirect your thinking, and change your perspectives where needed; to review your past and present and gain insights to help you plan and progress in your life. It can guide you to unveil your gifts, the good in you and the purpose of your life. This you do on your terms in your own rhythm – from your own DNA – from your truth. Through reflection you can experience the profound joy of self-discovery and mastery of your world.

When I assign a reflection exercise to my students they initially struggle with the concept. They stare back at me with blank faces as if to say: *"Really?"* The reason behind the blank questioning faces is because the subject is not only foreign to them, but also it is a resistance to do the strange task I am assigning. I help them to understand that this is a necessary task and one they will appreciate when it is completed. There is no escape from a 'reflection exercise' in my classroom. In fact, this is one of the very first standard assignments I give. I know that the reflection will loosen and open my students' minds. It will help to ground them in themselves and energize their learning. This always proves to be true.

Once my students have embraced the concept of 'reflection' and do the assignment, despite how foreign and difficult it may be for them, they inevitably open up and welcome it - like right-handed persons learning how to write with their left hands, and to perform the same tasks with the left hands that they had with the right hands for all their lives. Once students get beyond their angst and resistance and on the other side of the 'reflection' assignment they are surprised and amazed that they could do it. They are eager to report the insights they gained and the heightened sense of self they feel. Literally, the energy in the classroom shifts and is lifted. 'Lo and behold', they have been introduced to the ambidextrous mind! The students report how liberated they feel with the new knowledge they gained or just the expansiveness and self-confidence which came with exercising those new mental muscles. As one student put it, *"This exercise to reflect better acquainted me with myself and how I think. I learned what goes on inside me that I never realized."*

How to Reflect?

Self-discovery begins with stopping the external noise and activity to be alone with YOU to reflect. Every life needs reflection – without it is a recipe for madness! Reflection should be a part of your regular life and is most effective when it is. It can be done on a moment's notice when you recognize the need to step back from a situation to take it in; and it can be planned – with you charting out some specific time, be it several minutes, an hour, an evening, or a Sunday afternoon. It is as essential as breathing oxygen in and exhaling carbon dioxide out; it is as necessary as a massage that loosens and releases toxins from the body, and like restful sleep at the end of the day.

To reflect is to take an inventory of your thinking processes, to take a second look at how you behaved in a particular situation, to see in hindsight how you feel about what you did or did not do – and whether you might behave differently at a future time - perhaps to reach a different or better outcome. It is to see where you served yourself well or where you let yourself down, and where there is room for improvement. It is to track how your thinking is mirrored in your experiences. It is to mentally review your activities of the past day, weeks or months and see what insights surface. Or it is just to be still and quiet with yourself with no mental agenda and allow your mind to clear and wander and for something to come through. It is a process by which you can ask yourself some critical and private questions - engaging the counsel of your higher self. Questions have alchemical properties. Contained within a question is the seed to transform a situation or reality. Reflection is a time to ask questions – to cultivate that seed. Just mentally submitting a question to one's mind will naturally generate a relevant response. This is the alchemical process at work. When the response comes it might at times be difficult to accept - it may be contrary to what one expects. The responses may challenge a mindset, a decision, an assumption, or threaten to pull one out of their comfort zone. But responses are just that, they are there for consideration and can just hang and float or be acted upon - they are gifts of the reflective process. The responses are merely information. Allowing these to come through to be reviewed or considered keeps the channels open for more insights to appear, even delightful, uplifting ones. Gradually, in time, reflection enables one to become more adept at navigating his or her own mind and accessing the greater parts of their being – harvesting answers that could not come from any other place.

Reflection and Meditation

Reflection and meditation are two distinct modes of tuning within and consciously conducting inner-work. The two terms are often confused as being the same. However, these are different processes that complement each other. Reflection is a deliberate process to enhance your mental and consciousness capacities and to make informed decisions and choices; while meditation brings you into states of calm and peace, to groom and open your mind to receive insights. Meditation has its origins in eastern cultures and is widely accepted in western society. Meditation is a practice that we enter to relax, quiet, clear and rest the mind; and we do this usually by solemnly composing and positioning ourselves - closing our eyes and sitting still in a comfortable sustained position in an isolated area. In this regard meditation is a passive, receptive process, with the goal of reaching tranquility and relief from stress or an over-taxed mind. With meditation your mind becomes seated in the inner realms; it can be a beatific process to train and help you practice mental openness. When you meditate you are enhancing your mental acuity to tune into a higher wavelength of consciousness.

In meditation the mind has no real 'agenda' or target. The fact is that often, during meditation, thoughts and mental items intrude – making it hard to put the mind to rest. That is because these thoughts and mental items clamor for attention and crowd the spaces of psyche. These thoughts and mental items naturally need attention because these too, play a role in generating your experiences. However, meditation is not the time to entertain these. Such mental intrusions prevent one from stilling, quieting and resting the mind and from achieving a desired state of emptiness and serenity.

Reflection is a more active and determined process; the mind has an 'agenda' and a target. Reflection is exploring the inner sanctum of your mind – viewing and reviewing your thought processes in relation to your experiences; it is examining your emotional responses and triggers. Reflection is taking inventory – rewinding and playing back the tape on the day's events – remotely witnessing your past actions and behaviors, assessing your tendencies – even examining the thoughts and assumptions that you relied on during the day, or week, or month or year. The process can be clearing but done more keenly than meditation - like mental housekeeping. Reflection welcomes the intruding busy thoughts as information to be processed. It seeks to catch and speak to these and hear the messages these carry and reveal cogent meanings. Reflection can be done with eyes wide open, or while one is walking around or even engaged with others with the inner-eye turned on and tuned in. Reflection allows one to 'eyeball' what is happening around, within and about him and her. In reflection, one can step outside himself or herself to observe, analyze and better understand situations. They become the objective observer of their life and experiences - seeing what is there to see. In reflection one can see the blind spots, gaps and openings and next steps to take. One can see the subtleties at work that influence her and his life; one can engage their shadow.

Often reflection can be a prelude to meditation. It processes and clears the mental data - making the mind more receptive to peace and calm. This cannot happen the other way around; meditation cannot precede reflection if either process is to be effective.

Unplugging the Over-Externalized Mind

As stated earlier, most of humankind's problems can be solved if people can take the time to be alone with themselves. Our human progress is limited by our rote embrace as 'real' that which comes through our objective senses, and primarily because it *comes through our objective senses*. This tendency stifles the fullest expression, growth, evolution, and contribution of the human being. It is a limitation that is evident at both the individual level and with global collective humanity. The irony is that people spend most of their time in their minds, which is too often a default function of being human. The good news is that liberating ourselves from the over-externalized mind is simply unplugging that single cord and replacing the 'socket' of psyche with a multiple-surge power cord that allows equal access to inward and outward views. It is deciding in our awareness that 'over-externalized' is not what we wish to be nor is it the best way to be.

Reflection is a key tool to help generate the healthy shifts that are needed in the world today, and it should be a part of any curriculum for education, especially higher education. Moreover, reflection could be encouraged by business institutions and organizations to allow 'Mental Health' days off in balance with sick days; and ideally, reflection should be a value instilled in religious institutions by encouraging parishioners to literally heed the sacred scripts - to *"Know Thyself"*. There is no way around it, you need to 'reflect' on your way to becoming a more conscious being.

TOOLBOX

1. *Use Reflection as a Tool.*

   Make time to reflect. Make it a priority. Fit reflection into your life routine. Schedule a regular time to reflect. Take a step back from activity to do this. Enter reflection as a door you pass through to explore the existential questions in your life, and to know thyself.

2. *Be Receptive.*

    The mind earns by doing, the heart earns by trying. Come to the reflection process with the aim to receive – be receptive – open your mind and your heart. Reflection can prime you to take those 'mental leaps' that can be a part of the consciousness-raising process.

3. *See What Is There.*

    Put your fears aside. Do not be afraid of what you might find inside. Fear can only block and stifle you in this inner sanctum. Whatever you are going to see is there whether you choose to see it or not; and it is already directing your actions and shaping your experiences. Seeing it is like shining a flashlight on it. When you shine a light on something that is fearful or threatening you diffuse and demystify its power. On the other hand, you may be amazed with what you find. It is all useful information. See it. Nobody is looking at it in that private space and moment but 'you' anyway. This is between you and you.

4. *Practice Intentional Problem-Solving Reflection.*

    Bring questions to the reflection process. Make it a point to submit one or more question to yourself in your reflections and request and expect that answers, insights and solutions will come through. Purity of intention is essential to this exercise and is relevant to each person. Have the intention to access subtle information and insights. This will spark the alchemical process. Give yourself an assignment to work on in reflection mode. Start with what is troubling you, a situation you want to resolve or change – ask a question. Treat this as a creative and problem-solving session. The more you practice 'intentional reflection' the more useful information will come forth and the stronger your connection will become to the subjective reality and the knowledge that is there for you.

CHAPTER THREE

LOCUS OF CONTROL

If you want to hear God laugh, tell God your plans.

- Anonymous

Control can best be defined as the power to determine desired outcomes by directly influencing actions, people, and events. Control is something we'd like to have and may even think we have. However, inevitably we realize that there is no way to control all things in our lives. This is not to say that we cannot control anything; we must learn to step back and really analyze what we can and cannot control. This is important to consider in our growth towards an expanded consciousness.

The universally embraced and enduring 'Serenity Prayer' certainly applies here: *"God grant me the serenity to accept the things I cannot change; the courage to change the things I can; and the wisdom to know the difference."*

Within psychology, *'locus of control'* is an essential aspect of personality. The concept was developed originally by Julian Rotter in the 1950s. 'Locus of control' refers to a person's perception about the degree to which they have control over the outcomes of situations and events in their lives, i.e., they believe that they can control outcomes or that outcomes are determined by external forces such as fate, their concepts of God, or powerful others.

The term 'locus' implies a position, point or place, or where something originates or occurs. Hence, a person's locus of control may be internal or external. Psychologists, past and present agree that we are oriented to view the way control is manifested in our lives in two ways: Internal orientation and external orientation. With an internal 'locus of control' orientation we view the outcomes in our lives as being contingent on *what we do*. With an external 'locus of control' orientation we view outcomes as being influenced by *events beyond our control*. This explanation comes from psychologist Philip Zimbardo, *Psychology and Life, 1985*. A person with an internal locus of control believes that he or she can influence events and outcomes, while someone with an external locus of control blames outside forces for everything other than themselves.

Locus of control is a continuum – it is personal and different for everyone. No one has a 100 percent external or internal locus of control. Instead, most people lie somewhere on the continuum between the two extremes. It is best to have elements of both. What is key to know is the fact that we cannot get around the amorphous question of 'control'. When it comes to control, people seek it to manage their reality to achieve their desires. However, 'control' is *not* in any individual's power to possess or to wield. This assumption is an illusion. What people do have is the 'free will' to empower themselves in relation to control. To a large extent, people are healthier when they are poised to view and appreciate outcomes as much as possible as contingent on what they do - but not based on what they control. This perspective can be empowering and energizing. To a lesser extent one must surrender the illusion that he or she controls everything through their actions and accept that there are forces in their reality that exhibit significant control over the events and outcomes in their lives.

When it comes to locus of control, we need to be both internally and externally oriented. Again, we can *choose* our orientation about control through free will.

The term 'internal locus of control' is often used synonymously with 'self-determination' and 'personal mastery'. A person with an internal locus of control orientation is confident in their capacity to project a certain force of energy into the world to bring about the things and changes they want and need. In general, people with an internal locus of control tend to be content and closer to the fulfillment of their desires. A more internal locus of control is generally seen as desirable and enabling. However, an internal locus of control orientation is not necessarily inherently *good,* and an external locus of control orientation is not necessarily inherently *bad.*

There are subtleties and complexities to be considered regarding internal and external loci of control. There are drawbacks to both orientations when carried to an extreme. People who are overly internally oriented can become psychologically unhealthy and unstable. They can be hard on themselves and would constantly analyze what they did wrong – seeing more of the things that go awry that they brought about than the successes. This orientation places a person at risk of becoming hard-charging and negatively ego driven and driving themselves into the ground. Their internal orientation usually should be tempered with self-efficacy, and a realistic sense of their personal sphere of influence. Overly internalized people who lack these capacities in this regard can become neurotic, anxious, and depressed. On the other hand, people who have an overly external focus may come across as unmotivated, and as perpetual victims, exhibiting a learned helplessness; they are at the risk of leading aimless, failure-ridden lives. In either case, consideration needs to be given to such causal factors as environment, and circumstances (such as social privilege or disadvantage) in determining a person's locus of control orientation. The positives of either orientation is that with the dynamic levels of change, uncertainty and complexity in the world, having an external locus of control orientation gives you leverage by keeping you flexible, nimble, and adaptable; with an internal locus of control you have discernment, caution and prudence to navigate the same world terrain. One needs both.

The Impact of Interconnectedness

Because no one lives his or her life in a vacuum, the behaviors and actions of others indelibly impact our individual lives and our sense of control. A decision made by someone else, or others generates a chain of events that can impact and change your life. This is more common today because we are increasingly interconnected. We should expect this. When you think about it, our decisions and choices are to a great extent, influenced by those of others. Another person's decision and choices can and often do have a ripple effect and can impact how we think, feel and act. Internal locus of control means having a strong foundation that enables you to *discern* and *weather* this, and to adapt and use changes caused by another person to your advantage. For example: *A person who has been working at a job for several years and who may have reached a place of security and financial stability must retool or begin a job search when the company reorganizes, and that person's position is no longer needed.* Here, decisions made by others impact this person in a fundamental life altering manner. However, the decision on how to move forward, given the change is still within that person's locus of control. One never escapes the fact that they always have an 'internal locus of control' to use their free will to decide and choose.

Locus of Control Self Check

Ultimately, the need to have control can be replaced with an orientation to have both internal and external loci of controls.

Here are some vivid distinctions of both:

Those with a predominant internal locus of control:

Are prone to take responsibility for their actions.

Tend to be less influenced by other people.

Often do better at tasks when they are allowed to work on their own volition, having a strong sense of self-sufficiency.

Are prone to work hard to achieve the things they want; are often successful in their careers.

Are confident when faced with challenges.

Report being happier and more independent.

They tend to be visionaries.

Those with a predominant external locus of control:

> Can be easily engaged with the external environment and can exercise healthy aggressiveness and leadership.

> Can be sensitive to others and be strong team players.

> Have a strong capacity to 'let go'.

The following short assessment may help you ascertain where you are on the continuum of internal and external loci of control orientations.

Outlook 1

> *I often feel that I have little control over my life and what happens to me.*

> *It isn't worth setting goals or making plans because too many things can happen that are outside of my control.*

> *Life is a game of chance.*

> *Individuals have little influence over the events of the world.*

If the forementioned statements best reflect your view on life, then you tend to have an **external locus of control** orientation.

Outlook 2

> *If I work hard and am well-prepared and commit myself to a goal, I can achieve my heart's desire.*

> *Fate or destiny have nothing to do with me reaching my goals.*

> *Luck has little to do with my success; it's mostly a matter of my dedication and effort.*

If the forementioned statements best reflect your outlook on life, then you most likely have an **internal locus of control** orientation.

Knowing as much about your locus of control orientation as possible can be liberating; and with your free will you can elect to remain where you are on that continuum or modify your stance in relation to the world. This is what I call peak 'control'.

TOOLBOX

1. *Come to Terms with Your Locus of Control.*

   Continue to reflect and examine where your locus of control has been; and how this orientation has shaped your decisions and choices, and even your experiences. Know specifically, which situations are/were directly impacted by either internal or external locus of control. Challenge yourself to see how your choices and actions in this regard are controlling the outcomes in your reality.

2. *Shift Your Locus of Control.*

   If you find that you are overly externally oriented in your locus of control, and this has been problematic, shift to do some integrating with an internal orientation. Make the decision to cultivate your choices and behaviors from a more internal orientation where it is more helpful and to your benefit. Do the same if your locus of control orientation has been primarily internal and problematic.

3. *Continue to Monitor Your Locus of Control.*

   Locus of control orientation is not necessarily static – one goes back and forth between internal and external to some degree depending on the situation and one's level of comfort and habit. Know in the moment when you are operating in either internal or external mode. Do this particularly when you are met with challenges. Remind yourself that both orientations are important and relevant to certain situations and that you can use either, or both accordingly.

CHAPTER FOUR

OPTIMIZING ENERGY AND LIGHT IN YOUR LIFE

*Your world is a living manifestation of how
you have used and will use your mind.*
                            - Earl Nightingale

Thought is a living thing.
                            - Evelyn Pierson

The Energy Principle

Above and beyond skin, blood, and bone, you are an 'energy body'. Every life revolves around energy. Central to our journey in life is for us to become efficient stewards of the energy available to and within us to 'create and manifest' in a dense physical reality. We are tasked to do this amid all the distractions and constraints in the limited plane we inhabit. This is how we are designed. Raising your consciousness is essentially elevating your ability to be a conductor and producer of energy and to a high and higher qualitative degree!

Your consciousness is the ultimate agent in your personal growth and evolution. And consciousness-raising requires focusing on the energetic quality of your thoughts and your feelings. Countless research studies, books and journals have been produced on the importance of raising our consciousness and point to sound principles and dynamics involved in this noble undertaking, which pertain to energy. Energy is perpetually at work in every life. We are constantly interacting with the forces of energy and transmitting and receiving it. It is vital to comprehend and to understand the nature of the energies that shape and move in your life and your ability to work with these energies to generate the experiences you want.

Before there was anything, there was energy. Energy is at the core of all things, inanimate and animate – it is both substance and cause - it is an infinite intelligence. Nikola Tesla observed that the universe is made up of energy that vibrates at varying frequencies. Energy is a primary force that creates and generates through frequencies and vibrations. Energy is defined as *the capacity of a system or property to perform.* There are different kinds of energy: Thermal, kinetic, potential, electrical, chemical, nuclear and electrical. These are some of the energies germane to the physical plane. There are also other energies that exist and operate at the sub-atomic physics level – deeper than the physical plane.

Classical and contemporary scientists conclude that the basic element of matter is an 'energy consciousness' at the sub-atomic or quantum physics level. In the realm of sub-atomic physics, there is a form of energy that operates at a more subtle level than the typically known forms of energy mentioned earlier. This is 'elemental' energy, which does not exist or operate as things but rather as 'foci' of energy – or 'tendencies' of energy. Stay with me here.

It is the 'elemental' energy existing at the sub-atomic level which is motive and generates matter, therefore life and reality as we know it. This is also psyche - mental and spiritual energy, which is predominantly spiritual energy. The inherent nature of this spiritual energy is to expand, to create and generate. It is neutral, unbiased, and is ALWAYS operating in its tendency to expand, create and generate. We have access to this spiritual energy to expand, create and generate; we have this energy within us; and we are this energy. In other words, this spiritual energy permeates our consciousness, working with and through it; it is malleable, like clay to be shaped and directed by our thoughts and emotions and intentions. This energy is the medium through which we manifest our experiences and create our lives, either consciously or subconsciously. Unalterably and inevitably, we are all the time synced with this energy, whether we are aware of this and accept this fact or not.

Spiritual energy is the vehicle through which we direct our lives towards the object of our desire. The more we are conscious of this energy and how it is imbued in our lives, the greater the mastery we exert in our lives. To understand this energy and how you can consciously work with it, let us take a little excursion into the world of physics.

A Tiny Lesson in Physics

I will begin here with the Bottom Line, Part 1: *Every 'thing' is composed of atoms; at the sub-atomic level of the atom there is only 'possibility', not anything solid. This 'possibility' is 'energy'.* All energy manifests as frequencies and vibrations. This includes the physical and spiritual energies. Frequency is an invisible wave of energy that moves going in and out in cyclic patterns, away from a core and back again. Frequency is achieved when one pattern or cycle of vibration and oscillation occurs. Vibrations pertain to the number of movements or oscillations of energy particles. Both processes work in tandem. Science has long proven that energy is not manifested as a solid form but as a force vibrating at different levels. In essence, all matter and 'apparent' reality are composed of movements of energy that flash on and off, creating energy-frequency patterns. Energy is never at rest and is perpetually vibrating at different frequencies. That which appears as a solid is simply a collection of trillions upon trillions of atoms and sub-atoms vibrating at different frequencies. Frequency gives matter its uniqueness and characteristics - the faster the frequency the more solid and dense something appears. When our minds and bodies process the frequency patterns of objects, we see shapes, colors, and textures. The combination of frequency and vibration are some of the key energy properties that organize matter into shapes, proportions, dimensions, hues, etc. - giving matter tenable 'life'. This also applies to your own physical body! This scientific fact may seem incomprehensible because we are so wedded to the notion of physical manifestations of reality as being rock solid to the core.

Frequency has a multifaceted quality which is everywhere and inherent in all things. A mere apple is composed of rapidly occurring energetic frequencies. When you speak a word or take a breath, you are speaking and inhaling frequency. Whenever you listen to music, you are interacting with a frequency. When you think a thought or feel an emotion, you are experiencing these as frequencies.

Having Your Cake and Eating it Too!

The witticism that *'You can have your cake and eat it too'* is perfectly true and applicable regarding our relationship with energy. As we are energy conductors and producers, we are also essentially a composite of energy in terms of our physical body and in our consciousness. We are 'energy' that is also generating and creating energy. We are the paintbrush, we are the canvas, we are the hand that guides the paintbrush. We are the picture. What immense leverage we have over the circumstances of our lives!

Einstein's elegant groundbreaking theory that, *'matter and energy are the same and interchangeable'* cracked through all notions that we are exclusively one-dimensional sentient beings. It became clear that we are expressions of energy. And energy by its nature is multidimensional and cannot die but only transform. With this theorem, Einstein boldly opened the door for a deeper more intelligent conversation on the nature of being a human on this planet.

Taking Einstein's theorem further: *'Matter obeys the commandments of consciousness'.* Peering into the world of sub-atoms under the microscope, it became a new scientific fact that the tendencies, movements and the possibilities of the energy waves and particles were contingent on the mind (consciousness) of the observer! The endless gyrations and fluctuations of energy frequencies and vibrations preponderates in the physical world and in the stirring realms of consciousness; and these are swayed by states of consciousness, which is also energy. Matter is a denser form of energy with consciousness being a more refined form and expression of energy; they are composed of the same stuff and co-mingle in a sort of 'dance' – like a tango, a waltz or a rumba - with consciousness always leading the dance. Within the sub-atomic realm of consciousness this 'dancing' behavior and the frequency of movements of spiritual energy is contingent upon the current state of one's thoughts and emotions and other mental patterns. So, back to the 'possibility' at the sub-atomic level of the atom: Bottom Line, Part 2 - YOU CONTROL THAT POSSIBILITY.

There is much more to the mechanics of how energy as frequencies both represents and generates our experiences. Here, I would like to invite you to delve deeper into this area of quantum physics. It may continue to be an eye opener. For now, let us go on to discuss how spiritual energies help you to optimize *Light* in your life.

The Light of Consciousness

We are in a relationship with energy ad infinitum. Everything we do and experience requires some display, expenditure or give and take of energy - from getting out of bed in the morning, making a cup of coffee, having a conversation, thinking about your daily plans, enjoying a song, or feeling good about something. Energy is always moving on physical, mental, emotional and spiritual levels. As well, energy flows and vibrates on positive and negative currents.

As mentioned earlier, the way that energy is manifested to expand, create, and generate is unbiased and precisely neutral. Energy manifestations can be positive which enables you to increase your consciousness vibration, or it can be negative to decrease it. The way that your consciousness vibrates can be productive or counterproductive. It is a known scientific and medical fact that most illnesses are rooted in counter and conflicting energy frequencies in the body. Just as certain external electromagnetic energy frequencies are not in harmony with the body's frequencies and negatively affect the health of the body, certain internal thought/emotion energy frequencies generate unhealthy states of consciousness, which are not conducive to the constructive creation of one's life. Such frequencies disrupt the natural flow of your spiritual energy, causing it to swerve out of balance and become corrupted.

The higher your spiritual energies are vibrating, the more potent your ability becomes to expand, create and generate. This is because there is less density in your consciousness when it is vibrating at a higher level. This allows a wide space for the expanding, creating, and generating process to occur – like a horse galloping about freely in an open field. Raising your spiritual energetic vibration is equated to bringing more 'light' into your consciousness. Which is literally becoming more 'light' – meaning weightlessness as in not being burdened by the heavy ladened clutter of negative, counterproductive energies. Becoming 'brighter'. You know the difference in your 'being' when this state of consciousness is reached. This vaulted quality of consciousness can be *consciously* sustained to experience health in your psyche, and it puts you on the path of personal and life mastery.

Your thoughts and emotions are your link to the spiritual energies, which again, are always there at your disposal to direct as you wish – as the artist applying strokes to a canvas with a paintbrush. You are already 'painting the picture', whether you are aware or not; the important thing is to become increasingly *conscious* that you are engaged in this process – for most, if not all the time.

So, what is the 'light of consciousness'? And why seek it?

Light is an essential nutrient for the sustenance of life. We don't stop to think about 'light' per se, but rather, we take it for granted. However, we surely notice and would be hard put if the light were to go away. Think about the panic that ensues when there is a blackout, and the discomfort and insecurity we feel when the power goes out. When this happens, we forego everything to try to get the lights back on as quickly as possible. Or imagine a worst-case scenario if the sun did not rise one day because the earth rotated off its axis. In all such incidents the absence of light would be glaring and jarring – not only that, but it would also be destabilizing and impede activity and progress. This is because we know intrinsically that life cannot function without light.

Physics explains light as nature's way of transferring energy through space. It is a complicated process involving interacting electric and magnetic fields and quantum mechanics; however, simply speaking, *light is energy*. And this is the point to remember.

There is electromagnetic light in the physical realm, and there is spiritual light in the realm of consciousness which is a subtler form of the same electromagnetic energy; both operate on the same principles as physics. We need both and without these we are wandering and lost in the dark – literally and figuratively.

Natural light travels rapidly at a speed of 186,282 miles per second (or nearly 300,000 kilometers per second). This is truly fast! Light is finite and has a dual nature. That dual nature is expressed when light is both a particle (packets of energy – photons) and a wave. Photons of light contain varying amounts of energy – varying from X-rays (which carry a greater amount of energy) to optical photons to radio photons (with each carrying lesser amounts of energy). The differing quantities of energy that each photon carries produces different ranges of light. Light is also represented as a frequency wave. Hence, a beam of light is really a collection of little 'light bullets' or energy particles all strung together radiating from a source in 'waves'. Light waves move at different levels of frequency, with certain kinds of light having higher frequencies and certain others having low frequencies. The higher the frequency, the higher the vibration of energy it emanates. For example, in the optical light spectrum, blue light and red light are just 'light'; however, the blue light has a higher frequency of vibration than the red light.

What is important to know is that the physics notion of the nature of light and how it works is the same as the spiritual notion of light and how it works with and through consciousness. Light represents a *quality of energy*; at the sub-atomic level it also represents states of consciousness and operates in the same manner as it does in the physics plane. It cannot be identified, localized, or measured in the realm of consciousness; however, it is operative in the same vein as in representing energy moving along higher and lower frequencies or faster vibrations.

Light is health and progress. The brightness of light in your consciousness is equated to having a high physical/auric vibration. As *energy beings* we each own a certain vibration that emanates from within us. When we are vibrating at a high level, we keep the light in our lives bright – the higher the vibration emanating from us, the brighter the light. Vibrations are influenced by the consciousness we keep. When we think constructively and harbor such emotions as love, awe and gratitude we emanate a higher vibration and brighter light; this includes our behaviors of compassion, integrity, humility, peacefulness, non-judgment, and open-mindedness. Constructive thoughts, emotions and behaviors are in natural sync and harmony with the beneficent laws of the universe.

Light of consciousness is increased through the following:

1. Growing your mind and continually expanding it with knowledge. Keeping one's mind in ignorance is not happiness. Knowledge can be happiness.

2. Improving and managing the quality of the thoughts you hold onto and doing so on a regular basis.

3. Maintaining emotional health and maturity. This is also being emotionally responsible and intelligent.

4. Awareness and alignment with universal laws in such a way that you are more of a conscious proactive partner with these laws in orchestrating your life.

Being an efficient conductor and producer of energy helps you to optimize the light of consciousness in your life. The more 'light' you access and radiate, the more self-aware and effective as a human being you become. You can make the right choices; the right thoughts come to your mind; and the best ideas come forth. In the clearing that the light generates you can see farther and hear the subtle voices within you that can guide and connect you with openings and opportunities that move your life in the direction you want.

Energy and Vibration Management

Thoughts and Beliefs

The thought process controls electromagnetic spiritual energies. A thought is a collection of words in your mind on a given subject. Judgments are thoughts, criticisms are thoughts, reflections are thoughts, opinions are thoughts, assumptions are thoughts, ideas are thoughts. Thoughts come and go, and usually pass through your mind hundreds of times a day without you giving these any notice or attention or giving them a single thought – if I may offer a pun. And all thoughts are expressions of energy projected into the world to create our personal realities.

Beliefs are thoughts that have become affirmed from repeated use. Notice I said 'use' when referring to thoughts - because your thoughts do not belong to you. Beliefs are descriptions and deep convictions you have about something. Beliefs are not as easy to change as thoughts. They are fastened to your mind and become so much a part of your internal processes that you are hardly aware of these. Yet, beliefs also do not belong to you. However, beliefs still have much power. While all thoughts go towards the creation of your reality, beliefs escalate the manifestation process; this is because beliefs shape your intentions and over time become more concrete as 'values'. What you believe deeply is manifested into your personal reality. Like a tape recording, beliefs are programmed instructions that you energetically transmit into the world, and these instruct your decisions and choices. Your consistent, clear, and clean positive beliefs excite the sub-atomic atoms of your consciousness to a higher energy state. Examining and managing the thought, belief and even the feeling systems you *use* are at the root of optimizing light and the energy available to you.

Mental and Emotional Housekeeping

Thoughts and emotions have either positive or negative energy charges; we are always choosing one or the other - choosing detrimental over nutritious ones. Fear and negativity are lower energies and impulses that clutter, dominate, and crowd our psyche when we are not aware and guarding our inner life. These are like toxins that contaminate one's consciousness. A major step to having *control* is to order one's thinking. Raising one's consciousness begins in the private recesses of one's mind. If a person truly wants to raise his or her consciousness they must examine and re-train their mind and clear it of mental and emotional toxins and debris. Mental and emotional housekeeping means sifting through and arresting wayward thoughts, putting questionable emotional and mental habits in check to refine or discard what does not serve you, and which you decide not to *use* anymore; and then to retain and magnify those which are of use and serve you - and better yet, add new ones!

As sentient beings, we desire peace and happiness through personal fulfillment, calm of mind, and relief from fear and anxiety; we desire financial security, contentment, affection, freedom, control, wisdom, and health. At the same time, we are the chief engineers of much of the chaos, pain, obstruction, and turmoil in our lives, which adds to the uncertainty and sea of constant change we must traverse to reach the object of our desires. Our thoughts are the key instruments through which we create our experiences. Again, we do this as automatically as our hearts beat without our constant awareness; and this happens in accordance with the principles of energy described earlier. What we experience in large part stems from our states of consciousness. Expanding one's consciousness requires keeping a 'clean house' through the examination of the thoughts, beliefs, and emotions one habitually entertains in his and her psyche; and striving to maintain an inner life that is operating on higher thought and emotional vibrations and frequencies.

Often what we desire most is not compatible with the present state of our consciousness; and the consciousness that targets a particular thing or situation may not necessarily be conducive to receiving its desired 'object'. Minding the consciousness you keep is like preparing your living environment to receive much anticipated special guests. The internal housekeeping must be done to prepare and make the environment ready and fitting.

Free Will and Conscious Choice

As humans, at a soul/spiritual level we desire to receive all that the *light* is offering. And life is a series of choices we make in pursuit of light – happiness. Whether the choices we make are noble or corrupt our activities are made in pursuit of *light*. This light is manifested in various ways, such as in loving and rewarding relationships, prosperous careers, personal accomplishments and recognition, contentment, a happy family life, emotional connection and satisfaction, optimal health, financial security, knowledge, and wisdom. We access and work with an infinite reservoir of spiritual energies to obtain these things. The more consciously we manage energy and reflect light the more likely we are to achieve these things.

The fundamental choices we make daily either consciously or not, are on the kinds of thoughts and emotions we will entertain in our private mind and which we will project into the world. This is the platform, which is often the battleground upon which our pursuit of happiness is waged. And there are certain thought and emotional patterns that produce both healthy and unhealthy climates in the human psyche. Expanding consciousness means understanding and managing our mental and emotional climate day to day, hour to hour or minute by minute, until such time that you have achieved the climate most conducive to optimizing your access to light and the best energies to achieve the object of your desire.

Managing your mental and emotional climate is simply a matter of free will and choice, which springs from external and internal loci of control. We optimize our energy and light better from an internal locus of control because what we *can* control is the 'quality' of the thoughts and emotions we harbor. It is a proven fact of sub-atomic physics that certain thought patterns block light and weigh people down mentally, emotionally and spiritually – even physically and have them vibrating at low levels. These include, envy, cynicism, jealously, anger, resentment, self-doubt, and other negative emotions. Habitual anger and hate are two of the most destructive emotional patterns, with cynicism leading the way as a most counterproductive mental habit. These crippling mental and emotional habits impede one's ability to positively construct his or her life. An inbred state of fearfulness is a stubborn impediment to accessing and working constructively with the spiritual energies that are available to everyone. Conversely, it is a fact that a regimen of positive thoughts and emotions have the opposite effect.

Shifting from Reacting to Being Proactive

Conscious choice and free will always determine how we react to the myriad of events and impressions we encounter, and which keep coming at us. Just as we can discern and choose which thoughts and emotions serve us and which do not, we can apply conscious choice and free will to how we will or will not react to circumstances that are usually beyond our control. When you think about it, we are always tempted to react to something. This is because most of our behavior is reactive. Life is structured that way.

We tend to react mostly out of emotions. And because emotions do not belong to us we can choose to take on an emotion or not; and as well, we can choose to check, block, and neutralize certain ideas from taking hold in our psyche to influence us one way or another. You have that degree of internal control. Being less reactive is parallel to operating from an internal locus of control while reacting too much is parallel to operating from an external locus of control. When you react less you experience a greater sense of personal power and mastery. You are really 'lighter'. Raising your consciousness is neutralizing and rising above 'reactivity. It gives you leverage to be more of the cause in your life and less on the receiving end of persons, circumstances or situations that do not serve you and that you cannot control.

Reacting burdens you where you feel that you need to do something about everything that comes at you, when it is easier and healthier to just let things flow through you – becoming transparent. This does not make you wimpy or a patsy where conflictual situations are concerned, but smarter. Much of what we are reacting to depletes our energy and decreases our ability to receive light. Here are ways to shift from reactive behavior to being proactive and increasing your capacity to access light:

1. Reacting less to external events and situations in your life, not being an effect but a cause. Being discerning about what you will react to or not. When you react the situation or event controls you and you become the effect not the cause.

2. Surrendering the illusion of external control where this is relevant; and not habitually and automatically allowing outside forces to dominate and influence your state of mind and feelings.

3. Not exhibiting egocentric and self-centered behavior or pursuing ego gratification at all costs. These are just as counterproductive as thoughts and emotions can be and are projected to try to fill an 'empty vessel'. These are 'reactive' behaviors born out of low self-esteem and insecurity. These hinder a person from evolving and keeps them ebbing at lower levels of consciousness. These obstruct light and positive energy flow because these are heavy and non-generative. Being proactive is feeding your self-esteem in healthy ways. This keeps you stable and less likely to overreact.

4. Very key to optimizing the energy and light is to recognize when you have manifested something that you dearly wanted. Often our moments of manifestation slip by, go unnoticed and are taken for granted. Usually, we come to realize that something we wanted has come and gone or is almost passing by without our noticing and appreciating it. This is what I call the *"Uh Oh!"* factor - when we see sometimes too late, what we positively generated. It goes by without us recognizing and embracing it. We react after the fact that 'W*hat I was hoping to happen has already occurred'*. It is more energizing to acknowledge that: '*What I wanted to have is now happening and, in my life, now'*. Acknowledging in the moment what you are manifesting is being really proactive and

increases your continued ability to manifest and magnifies the energy and light coming to you. Reflection helps you to capture the moment when your manifestations are coming to life.

Resisting and purging negative thought forms and emotions, impulses and reactive behavior keeps spiritual light shining. Being aware while this is happening is a vital part of the process. Awareness and self-witnessing how your own processes are being re-fashioned - of how you are choosing to think, feel and 'react' differently increases your vibration.

Just as it is our nature to desire, *being 'receptive' is a natural state of being* for us, whereby we receive and experience light in the form of the things we desire, and that the universe is poised to 'give'. When you do the internal disciplined work of reviewing, cleansing and purging your thoughts, emotions, and reactive patterns you open yourself and are in your natural state to receive. The absence of the clutter of negative thinking, hard and heavy emotions, ego and self-centeredness and reactionary habits naturally opens you up to receive light. This is because you are releasing and holding on to less – you are opening a fist that was before clenched tight and hard.

A reflective lifestyle prepares you to do this level of internal work. With the increased self-knowledge that comes from a reflective lifestyle comes clarity, making you aware of the thoughts and emotions that serve you best; you are then more likely to use free will and conscious choice more automatically and with less effort. This moves you closer to manifesting the object of your desire.

When you put a desire into the universe to fulfill you have an obligation to cooperate with the universal forces to make this happen. This involves keeping the channels and pathways clear for the good you want to come through to you.

Embracing Problems and Obstacles

The venerable philosopher Hippocrates stated that: *"All the roads of learning begin in darkness and go out into the light."* Problems and obstacles bring us opportunities to better ourselves and generate light. The more barriers and challenges you have the more you can plug in and access light. When we fail to meet the problem or obstacle before us or recognize the opportunity to correct our negative behavior that it brings, the problem or obstacle becomes stronger; it will not go away. Or if by some chance it fades, we will inevitably face it again. Clinging to comfort zones to avoid the problems that were meant for us produces a momentary relief; however, this delay builds into more long-term and entrenched problems.

Problems allow us to use higher tools and learned skills to work through them, and it is often the case that only the use of a higher awareness and tools enables us to overcome these problems and obstacles. Life is a considerable classroom where lessons are learned - where problems and challenges are like taking a course that can teach and help us correct and transform attitudes and behaviors that work against us; and which are usually the cause behind the problem or obstacles we are facing. Problems test us to rise and flex blubbery or little used muscles of our psyche. We should welcome and embrace problems and obstacles, as indeed these will come. The greater the degree of change and uncertainty in our lives and the world, the greater the degree of problems and challenges we will encounter.

Problems and obstacles usually are designed to help you transcend certain counterproductive patterns in your psyche that block and stunt your growth. These may include:

1.   Being egocentric and self-centered.

2.   Habitual doubt and insecurity.

3.   Allowing the voices of the past and defeat to dominate you.

4.   Habitual anger.

5.   Laziness.

61

6.   Being judgmental.

7.   Self-aggrandizement.

8.   The impulse to criticize, gossip, and small-mindedness.

9.   The impulse to be controlling, and over-attachment.

10.   Guilt. Beating up on yourself. Being overly self-depreciating.

11.   Lack of confidence, choosing to play the victim.

12.   Selfishness.

13.   Being easily embarrassed and self-shaming.

14.   The perpetual need to be admired.

Again, your consciousness is the primary agent in your personal unfolding. You must be serious and responsible about what you do with it. Just as people choose to ingest nutritious foods, good water, and air, it is prudent to be mindful not to put anything into one's consciousness. The more one can transcend counterproductive habits of mind, the more clear their psyche will be, with open and widening channels to receive light.

The Pursuit of Happiness - Revisited

The subjective world is full of light! And we are in essence, beings of light desiring to re-connect with our source! When you reflect and become aware, you access this light. What we are all essentially seeking in life is LIGHT and by extension, happiness. The God of our hearts fosters the manifestation of our aspirations and desires that contribute to happiness. This is so because happiness that is based on a responsible life is the foundation for the soul's evolution.

TOOLBOX

1. *Monitor and Manage the Quality of Your Thoughts and Energy.*

   This is an intensive on the quality of your thoughts and energy: a) Through reflection, continue to become intimately acquainted with how you think, and how your thoughts shape your beliefs and direct your behavior. Focus on the qualitative nature of your thoughts. Go deep. Assess the nexus of your thoughts and your reality and the quality of energy you are projecting into the environment. Ask yourself: "Exactly what am I putting out into the world in this regard?" Keep in mind that thoughts are units of and qualities of energy. Know that you control this and can change this only when you know what is there. This should be easy because you, like everyone else, spend most of your time in your mind. Spend regular time assessing the 'quality' of the energy you are transmitting and in all that you do.

   b) In a separate process, continually monitor what you focus on and on the general mood of your consciousness. Assess the climate and quality of your inner life. Ask yourself: "How do my thoughts make me feel?" Focus on what you say to yourself - about yourself and others internally. Understand which voices and 'feeling tones' rule within you. Are you hopeful or pessimistic? Is the glass half empty or half full? While a thought is a temporary short-term thing, patterns of thoughts and beliefs indelibly determine the health and climate of your consciousness and inner life over time. Come to know the quality of the thoughts and even the emotions you entertain on a regular basis.

   Additionally, there is always a direct correlation between the quality of your thoughts and energy and how this blocks or opens access to light; this is something to assess in your reflections.

2. *Revamp Your Thought Habits and Patterns.*

Thoughts need cleansing and refreshing just as we brush our teeth and shower in the morning. All of our life experiences have their origins in a thought. That thought that occupied your mind over time became a belief; that belief which hardened over time became a value; and that value informed and shaped your experiences and reality. Keep this causal sequence top of mind. As humans we have the privilege to change out of one 'self' and into another. You can restore your consciousness. If the quality of your thoughts and feelings, hence the quality of energy they project and feed your consciousness are problematic and not useful, you can revamp these. You can literally shift the quality of the energy you project, and which fuels your consciousness. You do this in the same manner that you change clothes daily. Here is how you might proceed:

Identify an experience – perhaps a problematic recurring pattern, one that you may want to eliminate from your life. Now trace that experience or pattern back to the incipient thought that generated it or to the thought or emotional habit that fuels it. Choose immediately to change, or eliminate that thought/emotional habit, and to monitor when it shows up in the future. What makes this easier is to simply affirm that: 'This thought/emotion does not belong to me. I now release it.'' This level of awareness requires discipline, presence, and repetition, and above all honesty, which over time will reshape your experiences. With practiced reflection and clarity on your locus of control you can sense when these habits and patterns occur and block you, and you can choose to change them. In time, this practice can become second nature, and a bonafide game changer. In the same vein, think about the opportunities that came to you and trace these back to the thoughts or emotional habits that generated these and continue to project these kinds of thoughts and emotion.

3. *Deepen Your Knowledge of Your Sources of Energy.*

   Become intimately knowledgeable of the contexts, situations, kinds of people, as well as your own attitudes and behaviors that energize you in the most helpful ways. This knowledge is best discerned in the Introversion/Extroversion temperament scale of the Myers-Briggs instrument. These temperaments have nothing to do with being either shy or a social butterfly, but rather from where you are inclined to get your energy. For example, people who are mostly INTROVERTED get energy from within themselves. They typically can get drained from too much social activity and require time alone to recharge their batteries, so to speak; whereas the EXTROVERTED person thrives and gets energized through social interactions. Neither is good or bad, it is simply a matter of where people source out their vital energy.

4. *Look for the Good.*

   Take your self-check a step further to examine how you look at others. Do you habitually look for faults in others, do you seek to criticize or judge? Or do you see the good and what is right in others more than their faults? This also determines how you energize yourself. Train yourself to notice and catch those negative thoughts of judgment, cynicism, criticism which are all too often knee-jerk responses to situations that we internally feel threaten us and which might stem from how we are programmed to be fearful. These kinds of thoughts are not healthy and hurt you more than the people you may project them onto. Again, these cut you off from the supply of light that you want to access for your life.

5. *Manage Energy Exchanges Rule #1.*

   Understand that all conversations are exchanges of energy. Monitor the language and words you use and the contexts in which you use these words as much as you can. There are certain words that block energy and light in social exchanges. Some of these are: BUT, MIGHT, MAYBE, and CAN'T. The use of 'BUT' is resplendent in our world society. 'BUT' is one of the most obstructive of all words. It halts movement in the conversation and the possibilities that may extend from that conversation. Energetically, 'BUT' is a light blocker. Understand that whenever this word shows up in a conversation it negates everything said that precedes it. Minimize your use of this word. Replace it with 'AND' where you can.

For example: Instead of saying "I understand and sympathize with you, BUT I think there is another way to look at this." Say: "I understand and sympathize with you, AND I think there is another way to look at this." See the difference and how this shifts the quality of the exchange? Getting "BUT" out of the way serves you more than the other person. Because it keeps openings for light and energy to come through to you.

6. *Manage Energy Exchanges Rule #2.*

   When interacting with others be aware of how energy is exchanged. Make sure that you are not giving good energy away towards bad energy. And vice versa, make sure that you are not being an 'energy vampire' - sucking the energy out of the conversation and from any constructive exchange with other persons. At the same time avoid people who are habitually energy vampires as much as you can. Interact in a way that ensures that the energy exchanges are balanced. Also make sure that the quality of energy you take in from others is healthy and beneficial.

7. *Manage Energy Exchanges Rule #3.*

   Avoid being on the defensive as much as possible. Anytime you are on the defensive you are giving away your energy in an unhealthy way and weakening your connection and access to light. Instead, be neutral where you can and strive for being on a healthy offensive. When it comes to conflict situations or disagreements, monitor the degree to which you are on the defensive or the offensive. A positively offensive stance guards and retains your energy, whereas a defensive stance depletes your energy. Being in this awareness in and of itself enables you to make a positive choice in the moment on how you will manage and maximize your energy.

8. *Practice Purposeful Visualization.*

   This will always be true: The visible emanates from the invisible; and all things created by human beings are manifestations of how and what they think; and a thought form whether individual or collective, positive, or negative, will manifest at some point in time on earth. By visualizing an event or situation that you strongly desire to come true, you create in the cosmos the spiritual conditions for its manifestation. Visualization, also called mentation, is a deliberate energetic process that you control. In this process you create a 'thought form' by holding a mental image of what you desire and infuse it with your strong feelings; this 'thought form' under the impulses of natural, universal, and spiritual laws generates the influx necessary for it to materialize. It is best and more potent to visual the 'fulfillment' of the desire as though it has already come to past, and when it is legitimate and in harmony with your highest good. Visualize with the deepest conviction that you DESERVE what you are visualizing, and that it is right.

9. *Choose to Be in a State of Gratitude.*

   Gratitude is a most revolutionary posture to assume with all that is going on in the world and perhaps around you. It lifts, energizes and brightens like an instant tonic! Make it a habit to be in a state of gratitude. A perpetual state of gratitude keeps the portals to light open to you. Gratitude is also an excellent and a healthy replacement for cynicism. It can be as simple as counting your blessings and saying, "Thank You", silently within yourself or aloud - as often as you can, in times of trouble, in times of bliss, and just because . . .

Kindly refer to the Simple Energy Awareness and Management Spectrum in the Appendix of this book.

Formula 9

CHAPTER FIVE

COSMIC RELATIONSHIPS

I have learned silence from the talkative,
tolerance from the intolerant and kindness from the unkind.
I should not be ungrateful for those teachers.

- Khalil Gibran

Relationships are Vehicles for Personal Evolution

Relationships have a singular and profound influence in our lives. Much of what we do, and experience involves and depends on people! We need others. Much of our effectiveness, successes and happiness relies on our ability to form, manage, and sustain relationships; and as such, much of our sadness and failures are connected to relationships. This applies to personal and professional relationships. For many and perhaps most people, belonging and having close relationships is the *object of their desire* over a lifetime. Relationships are vehicles through which we come to know ourselves, live out our lives and evolve to higher levels, and to achieve our ideals and potentials. In this sense, relationships are like cars – which help us get from one place to another safely and intact. If the engine does not work the car will not run. Likewise, with relationships, you will experience the counter effect if the major relationships in your life are not working.

Relationships are connections with and among people through blood, values, interests, history, or shared circumstances. Those relationships that truly support us are the foundations for a strong and well-lived life. Healthy relationships require effort and should not be taken for granted – but rather nurtured and sustained where this is possible.

The term 'cosmic' refers to something related to the expansive universe and is of great importance. In this sense, all relationships are 'cosmic' because relationships are intrinsically, invaluable vehicles for the growth and evolution that is at the core of our journeys in life. Any relationship and connection with another is of significance. Relationships essentially, bring us into existence by reflecting us back to ourselves; and it is from relationships that we extend ourselves into the world to test, demonstrate, and make manifest and apparent how we are learning, stretching and growing - or not.

Relationships are governed by universal laws. The universe is in a constant state of growth and expansion; and so are we because we are made of the same star stuff that composes the universe. We are always expanding in some way towards our better selves or otherwise. Each encounter you have with another person, whether as part of a family circle, an intimate or work relationship, or how you acknowledge a passing stranger on the street is an episode in which you extend yourself for better or worse. Every human contact impacts your growth and evolutionary process to larger and smaller degrees. This is the nature of all relationships. This is happening with and without your conscious awareness.

There is very little you can do or achieve in this life that does not involve people. The relationships that you have and will cultivate will matter in your life. These relationships are ones that you chose up to now and will choose; and they chose and will choose you. The relationships in your life at this time will impact you emotionally, mentally, financially, physically, spiritually – even soulfully. These relationships will lift you up or bring you down – or both.

Relationships are inherently emotionally-based. There is no way around this, even for professional ones. It is at the emotional level where we are the most vulnerable. Relationships are the source of most human pain, hurt, disappointment and abuse. Conversely, relationships are the sources of our greatest happiness, comfort, and nourishment. *What is true for all people is the need to feel safe and validated.* Relationships are the primary places we can experience the kind of safety and validation that feeds our soul and sense of well-being.

Family, Friends and Lovers

Family moves us; it consumes us. Your biological family is your first 'cosmic' relationship. You were born into it. It happened to you. You are genetically tied to family. It was within the family structure that your ideas about yourself were formed, and when you were most impressionable. This is the relationship which shaped your sense of self that remains with you as an adult, and it will remain with you throughout your lifetime. Your present thinking and feeling patterns were influenced and can be traced back to the family unit.

Because family is your first relationship, it is your most vital and enduring one. Ideally, for this reason our introduction to life through family should be loving and nurturing. It should nourish and support a person to grow well in all levels: physically, mentally, emotionally, and spiritually. Your most powerful growth and learning are spawned from your family experience. Impressions from childhood experiences are energetically programmed and infused in the memory and conduct of your cells. It is wonderful when a person can contribute much of how they are thriving in life to the suckle and sustenance they received in the family womb. And it is difficult to shift out of familial conditioning that might not serve one as an adult. However, this is possible. Family conditioning is in your cellular memory and can at best be managed rather than dislodged. If your upbringing was done with care, you are blessed and have leverage to pursue your life without the hinderances and obstacles that non-caring upbringing generates. Yet still, the most powerful growth can come from working through negative upbringing and toxic family relationships. Your reflections can reveal a lot to you about the nature of your connection with family and how early impressions from family are still with you and may be influencing your decisions, choices, and aspirations.

Family is as family does. A family's essential role is how it influences and shapes your life. There are other kinds of families, having nothing to do with sharing the same blood. Other than a biological mother or father, you can have a relative or friend who acts as a guardian. You can adopt a 'sister', 'brother' 'aunt' or 'uncle' from among your special friends. As you continually move and grow into the world, your family will expand to include your closest friends, teachers, and mentors. What matters is the core of love and support you receive from your family – whether they are biological or generated by your choices.

Friends are just as important as family. Where our biological family introduces us to the world, friends play a major role in lifting and spiriting us along our paths. Friendships are also relationships that reflect us back to ourselves. Friends meet us as we are 'becoming' in adulthood and gradually supplement and/or replace family ties and closeness. Friends tend to know us in ways that family cannot. We tend to share more aspects of ourselves with friends than with family. Friendships allow us to bring, reflect, and extend more of ourselves into this world.

Relationships with family, friends and lovers are powerful sources of love. Without love we cannot blossom and flourish into our truest selfhood. It makes us stronger emotionally, mentally, and spiritually when we can become a singular companion and support to another human being. 'Love' relationships are those where people share and exercise a commitment to one another's happiness in a manner more intimate than with family and friends. It is heaven when this is real between people. This refers to marriages, partnerships, courtships and romances. It is through these relationships where one can have the deepest experience of love - of loving and being loved, of belonging and being validated and 'brought into life' through love. Love of this kind energizes a life in a most profound way. Relationships, as described in Maslow's Hierarchy of Needs, is the third level of motivation that most people strive for, and once reached, they do not tend to aim or gravitate to higher motivations. Why? Perhaps because when we are loved, that is 'all important' and completing - sometimes more than the need for recognition, achievement, or personal actualization. The deep need for belonging and connection and to 'be in life' is fulfilled in personal relationships.

The Energy of Relationships

Just as we need food, water shelter, and affection to survive we need the energy that relationships constitute. Going back to the energy principles in Chapter 4, energy is the essential ingredient of all life. Without energy, life is not. Relationships are primary sources of energy for every human being. This energy comes from family, friends, lovers, associates, and colleagues, and even strangers we meet along the way. Just as we are always conducting the flow of energy in our lives as explained in Chapter 4, we are always conducting energy in and through our relationships. The objective is the same: To be effective conduits through which positive energy flows and to access and sustain as much 'light' energy in our relationships as possible with others.

Humans are not meant to do this life alone. However, we do need to consciously cultivate the right relationships to maximize the energy that relationships can provide us. There are relationships that can support and help you to grow and build your life, and there are relationships that can break your life down. It is the quality of energy that sustains or breaks down relationships. What really puts quality in relationships and intimate communications is when the parties are actively available to one another and which is made apparent through subtle signs such as: A certain kind of look, the drawing in of the breath in the act of listening; an encouraging gesture; or a silence that invites another to keep on going. All of which are refined expressions of energy. At the heart of failing relationships is an imbalance in how the energy is exchanged. Someone is taking more energy than he or she is giving; or someone is transmitting negative counterproductive *detractive* energies to the other person, causing the energy between them to be stuck, un-flowing or toxic, thus, causing pain, upsets, alienation and the sort.

Light and Dark Energy in Relationships

We need the energy that is always present and is exchanged between individuals in all contexts of relationships. We may not see this energy or be aware of it, however, it is ALWAYS there - flowing to and from individuals in every human encounter and exchange. And just as there are positive and negative currents of electrical energy traveling through wires, there are also light and dark waves of energy traveling between and among people - all the time.

Relationships that reflect light are those where individuals are compatible, feel validated and supported, and 'relate' in harmony with one another. They engage in an energetic exchange that encourages, lifts, and nourishes growth and well-being for the other. This kind of 'relating' is done with a natural inbred ease, or with a conscious and positive intent and effort. The result is the same, which makes plenty of room for light. Here, like attracts like. On the other hand, it is a universal principle that darkness seeks the light - energetically.

Nowhere is the force of darkness seeking the light more apparent than in relationships between individuals. In relationships there are *energy vampires* and *light killers* - those who prey upon and draw light energy from the other in unhealthy ways for their own sustenance. This kind of behavior can be done consciously or subconsciously - however, it is *felt* by the other person they are acting upon and it is damaging to the relationship. One of the most destructive forces is a wounded or broken person who voraciously feeds on other people's positive energy and light, or projects negative energy onto others. This is a way that this person becomes energized. These people are *energy vampires* or *light killers* or both. The difference between the two is subtle. Energy vampires are people who take more energy from the relationship than they give, and habitually drain energy from others. These people sap and deplete light from relationships through personal attacks, whining and complaining, habitual cynicism, criticism, negating, being judgmental, and incessant bragging and grandstanding; they 'suck' life by showing no support, and having control issues; they are chronically condescending, invalidating

74

and dismissive - even emotionally and physically abusive. They are self-centered and are usually grabbing all the attention to themselves - tearing other people down to build themselves up. Light killers are energy vampires on steroids, having the same behaviors, however with more intent and force. With intent, they use and treat people poorly as a rule. It appears that they are on a mission to destroy other people and can upset and ruin a chain of lives - even through the generations. They feed on the negative circumstances they generate. Light killers can distract you from focusing; they consume the energy you need for your life, and at worst, they can break your spirit. Energy vampires and light killers can be found in families, among friends, and in marriages and partnerships. You might have witnessed as I have how people's light was dimmed or snuffed by these predators. And light can always be turned back on.

All relationships thrive on light energy. You have the power and the free will to optimize the light energy that enters and sustains your relationships and keep it radiant. Growing your consciousness may at times require your willingness and ability to let go of certain kinds of relationships and people - energy vampires and light killers.

Validation as Sustenance in Life

A universal key to understanding relationships and cultivating positive and sustained relations is staying in the awareness that people need *validation* by being acknowledged and respected. Validation is as essential to our sustenance in life as is food, affection, shelter, rest, even pure love. When the exchange of energy between people is mutually validating, be it within a family, intimate partnership, friendship or in a business context the relationship is positively charged to be fulfilling and a haven for growth and expansion, productivity and progress, and just plain feeling good.

Here is a favorite example in this regard that I like to share: The northern Natal tribe in South Africa commonly greets one another by saying: *"Sawabona"* which means *"I SEE YOU."* In response the other says *"Sikhona"* which means *"I AM HERE"*, which is to say: *'When you see me you bring me into existence'*. This tradition of honoring the 'other' goes

75

to the very core of what validation means among humans. Validation is a form of love that we give causally to anyone. Validation is an even higher expression of love than sexual intimacy – because it does not come from the body but from one's purest intention and from the spirit, and it does not require that the giver and receiver are in a close relationship. It is a noble energetic expression that passes from one person to another – as an irresistible gift from the heart. Like the Natal tribe, when you validate another person, you bring them into life; subsequently, validating and treating people well is highly energizing for both the sender and receiver because the energy that is being transmitted both ways is positively charged and nourishing.

Validation is a form of the positive *light* energy that transmits from one person to another, just as criticisms and 'put downs' are forms of negative energy that go from one person to another. As humans and as energy receptors - we take in, hold, integrate, and harbor the expressions and the qualities of energies that are extended to us from other people. That is why love and support energizes and makes us happy, and abuse and rejection de-energizes and brings us sorrow, misery and pain. Growing your consciousness means to be vigilant about the quality of energy you are directly transmitting to others as well as the kinds of energies you are receiving from others. Always!

Karmic Relationships

Again, relationships are the primary vehicles through which humans can evolve to higher levels. 'Karmic relationships' are the ones that bring you the most learning and growth no matter how painful or fulfilling the relationship might be. These are the relationships that have a dramatic influence on you and can boost and accelerate you forward or drag you way down. Family, in and of itself is a karmic relationship, and so are most intimate and romantic relationships. However, karmic ties and destinies bring people together in love relationships more than with friends and family. In karmic 'love' relationships individuals are attracted or better yet, 'compelled' to be together out of some unspoken but subliminal understanding that they need one another at that juncture in their lives; most likely to work though, express or unfold aspects of themselves in a close and intimate *journey* with one another or to birth something together. It is also in these close love relationships that karma is generated - both positive and negative. The individuals' awareness of the karmic ties they share, and the role karma might play in their coupling can deepen the relationship and strengthen their bond.

Karmic relationships are charged and often irresistible. These were *really* meant for you – which can be positive or negative. These relationships may challenge and require you to work through some essential aspect or quality of your 'self' to learn, grow and evolve. You can move through and release 'negative' karmic relationships only after you have met the challenge or trial it has reserved and presented to you. Whatever the test or challenge might be, it is something that you can come to know and understand through reflection and self-knowledge.

Here's this. *In the movie: 'The Defiant Ones', there were two escaped prisoners who were also chained together at their wrists. One was a racist white man who repeatedly called the other black man "Boy"; both were filled with a rage stemming from their pasts and projected an old hurt and anger on to one another – they hated each other. The situation that had them chained together was intolerable. But their common goal was to find their way to a free life. During the experience they fought, cursed, and struggled against each other while fleeing from the prison authorities and their dogs. The chain forced them into a tight closeness with each other during their ordeal, which by happenstance allowed them to get to know one another, to tell their stories and bond in such a way that they ultimately made sacrifices to keep one another free - even after they found a way to cut off the chains that bound them. These men grew through that fateful experience. In the end, they were less agitated and unperturbed when they were eventually caught by the authorities. The foot race was over, but they had found a new freedom - through each other they had begun the journey to free themselves from their painful pasts and the blind rage their pasts wrought for them both. With these two men, the fears they brought into their initial encounter was masking something they needed to confront within themselves, with and through one another - and only by doing that they were made 'free', in another sense of the term.*

Learning and growth are the guiding principles in any relationship. Keep in mind that your 'entity' chose the family you were born into for the same reasons - for learning and growth. Many of the relationships and people coming into your life now are karmic relationships. These are meant to spur your growth and personal evolution. Some of the relationships coming to you are *decoy* relationships – meaning they are not karmic, but there to frustrate and pose obstacles to your growth – yet these also serve a vital purpose. These test you. One false move can cost you and deter you from your path - putting you off course. These decoy relationships reflect to you the lessons you need to become a better person. These bring forth the obstacles through which you must push through to growth. This is likened to a baby pushing through the mother's womb to be born. When you are cleared of the attitudes and habits that tainted and made your past relationships difficult and you have 'tools' and understanding of your own growth processes these *decoy* relationships cannot deter you. In fact, you may 'see these coming'. You will begin to attract more easily what I call the *wondrous* relationships. These are the relationships that you earn yourself into by passing the tests and learning *your* lessons; and in which you can stretch out and apply what you have learned and fully experience the joy and happiness that comes from this.

You will be experiencing more karmic relationships because the extreme times we live in today require growth and evolution of humans more than ever before. And with each relationship comes the inevitability that you will be generating positive or negative karma which will be meted out in time. So, as we need relationships for validation and sustenance, it is prudent to be mindful that we also need relationships to grow and evolve - which again, is the primary purpose of relationships. Striving to bring one's best 'self' to any relationship and encounter offsets negative karma - from family to friends, to lovers, to the clerks at the bank, to the person who checks one out at the grocery store - even the company rep who is trying to answer one's questions or sort out problems on the phone. This is vital in those relationships, whether one choose to engage them or not.

When it comes to having those loving romantic relationships and personal companionships of our dreams, one should try to make themselves ready before entering these. Sometimes it is wise to go 'solo' for a spell to better know oneself and work on inner issues, which if left unattended can sabotage and thwart a close and desired relationship.

At this point in time, humans cannot afford not to grow and evolve collectively beyond the traits that have brought us this far and which have generated the present state of the world. Collective karma? Yes, there is such a thing, and that is another book. For our purposes here, modern generations value and cherish relationships at a more spiritual and soulful level - more than prior generations. I personally believe that this is because the 'new people' are differently 'wired' and already tuned in to the truth about the 'cosmic' nature of relationships; and because they are the harbingers of the new ways of thinking and consciousness which is making its way into the world.

Maximizing Your Relationships

Quality over Quantity

Connecting with others is not just accumulating contacts and a host of friends. It is about choosing quality over quantity. The best relationships are built on a foundation of mutual respect, integrity, the exchange of ideas, common interests, support and for certain: validation. These are the kinds of relationships that foster greater and more satisfying growth. Good quality relationships amplify one's life.

Indelible Connections

We are connected. All experiences of pain and joy can be traced back to some connection with others. When you think of something that made you very happy and you found fulfilling, you can most likely trace it back to a connection you had with another person or persons. This is because at a fundamental level we are connected and the things and experiences you want are achieved through a connection or a sequence of connections with others. It's just a matter of degree.

Connections have meaning and possibilities, this includes those that are familial, professional, even chance encounters. Relationships and casual encounters can lead to breakthroughs and doors opened to opportunities one might not have imagined. From casual encounters one might get clues, and helpful bits of information, insights, or another contact or a direction that one needs to take. These encounters should not be taken for granted.

When it comes to relationship building and support, there is a 'feel good' principle involved in most newly formed professional relationships - those which are work or career related. In most professional situations people respond positively and help and support those that they feel good about. Employers hire people with whom they are comfortable; people mentor or invite those into their inner circles with whom they can relate and share interests. Contracts are awarded this way, as well as jobs. When people need services, they tend to ask a trusted friend for a referral to someone they know and trust rather than select randomly from a public database. This is why close relationships and tangential encounters require our attention and showing up with our best selves.

The Best Control is No Control

This takes us back to locus of control. Looking inward to change oneself can be far more challenging and arduous than attempting to control other people and manipulate the external environment; and trying to change the world is also a classic distraction from working on oneself. Therefore, people tend to avoid looking within and instead project their desire to control outward which is another folly of the 'over-externalized mind' we spoke of earlier. From our internal locus of control orientation, we get clear that we do not and cannot control other people. To think that this is possible and to attempt to do this is delusional, foolhardy and energetically speaking, trying to control other people depletes the energy and light you need in your life.

It is more empowering and personally effective to be clear that you can only control what you think, feel and how you react – that your locus of control is primarily in the realm of your choices and behaviors. Clarity that you can control YOU and not others exerts confidence and more magnetic energy. This energy can positively charge your relationships with others and bring about the kinds of outcomes you might have thought could only be achieved by trying to exert control over the other person.

Understandably, we live in a world with imperfect people, including ourselves. Other people's imperfections, issues and 'drama' adds to the frustrations we experience in personal and professional relationships. Ironically, this also makes life more interesting and sets the stage for our own personal growth and evolution. However, we are stronger when we stay tuned into the understanding that our locus of control is within ourselves, not others. Maximizing relationships means working within yourself - staying aware of your truest locus of control. Because you are always choosing how to manage yourself within relationships, this is the strongest and most strategic vantage point for you in relation to others. From this place you can influence others without trying to control them and which works better for all concerned. When we allow ourselves to do this, we can see ourselves better through others.

Because relationships mirror what is important to a person and in what ways they may need to grow, one can 'willfully' learn something about themselves through a relationship - any relationship can become a learning forum. Perhaps the need to try to exert control over others is telling one something about oneself. The negative traits one spots in others might reflect one's own negative traits, as well as the positives. One might see that there are certain 'people' skills that one needs to develop and deploy to bring more empathy into his or her relationships. From one's internal locus of control one can see and understand these, and other dynamics of the relationship and subsequently make better informed choices on how to change oneself to influence, work with or just 'be' with others. And when a person changes themselves, they are helping to elevate the entire world.

Overall, getting the most out of relationships requires a heightened level of personal awareness and accountability. Prudence and the best 'control' lies within one's personal sphere of influence.

Choice and Discernment

You choose how you are going to conduct the relationships 'assigned' to you. It is important to keep in mind that most of the people you encounter are, perhaps like you, challenged in some manner and about something. People have more and a different strain of problems than prior generations. Also, the social index of fear is higher than it has ever been – infecting people with stress, anxiety, and poor people skills. Civility seems to be on the decline. Fear darkens access to light that all people need and gives rise to non-productive and destructive behaviors. Life in today's world makes it essential to be highly discerning about who enters your sphere. One does not have to accept anyone into her and his circle of life.

Relationships, good and bad ones, are a huge part of what happens to us. The people we meet on our paths are agents in the construction of our lives. And vice versa! With today's lifestyles and challenges, one needs to know how to make things happen with and through people. It is also prudent to distance oneself from those who *"Don't know"* and who *"Don't want to know"*. These people either overtly or covertly, can deter and steer others backwards - putting them on a course to 'devolve'. Therefore, careful attention must be given to the people you allow to enter and participate in your circle life. Notice I said, 'allow' because you have more control in this choice now as an adult than you had as a child or young person. You can exercise greater control in having the healthy and supportive relationships you need to learn and grow and develop.

Additionally important is how to engage others – how to 'show up' in all relationships. For relationships are a two-way street. The way you choose to relate to someone else will determine how that person will treat you, most of the time. Relationships are indelibly about chemistry - expressed in the quality of the energy that is exchanged between people. People share and connect on the same wavelengths, with some better than others. This is normal and important to recognize. One's ability to be aware and discern the subjective and energetic information that always exists between and among people will help to promote helpful and healthy relationships.

TOOLBOX

1. *Know Thyself – Know Your Needs.*

   You spend most of your time in your mind. And that makes it natural and necessary to get to know yourself. The better you know your needs and what is best for you in relationships the more harmonious and fulfilling the relationships you choose will be. With self-knowledge you are better able to discern what works for you and what does not when it comes to relationships. Reflection allows you to take a good look at yourself – to take inventory to know how you function inside and out. Know your standards and boundaries, what you expect from yourself and in turn what you expect from others.

2. *Value the Relationship as a Sacred Place for Personal Growth.*

   Personal growth and improvement spans a lifetime and opportunities for this abound in your relationships. Approach relationships with this in mind, valuing these as spaces where you can harvest the best parts of you. You might want to do a retrospective on past key relationships through this lens. Going forward, know your growth needs and how a relationship with another and others can support these, and vice versa. And if you can openly talk about these things with another, you are well ahead!

3. *Let People Be Who They Need to Be.*

   Refrain from trying to control others. You cannot control other people. Let go of this tendency if you have it. If someone is in your life that you are trying to control, that person is probably not meant to be in your life – maybe it is not a match of interests or values. People belong to themselves, even in the most close and intimate relationships. The goal where differences are concerned is to find a happy medium that does not necessarily compromise the parties involved.

4. *Let People Make Their Own Mistakes.*

   Monitor the tendency to race to judgments or to hold others to yours or unrealistic standards. If they make mistakes or fall short of your expectations, understand that they are on their own journey to learn, grow and evolve – to access more light whether they are conscious of this or not. Let them learn and in the way they are meant to do so.

5. *Let Go.*

   Relationships are where we exercise most of our emotions and are at our most vulnerable. We need to feel safe in relationships more than in any other aspect of our lives. This is also where the things that can and do go wrong can knock us off course and cause us to lose our footing. Anger and resentments can and do arise; and when these become chronic and enduring, let go. Resentment is like taking a poison and expecting the other person to die. Resentment also blocks the light you need in your life to illuminate your path.

6. *Minimize Your Expectations of Others.*

   Be conservative in placing expectations on others. High expectations can and often do lead to disappointments; this can be de-energizing. Remember, you are also dealing with others who may struggle to live up to their own expectations. Minimize and/or be realistic with your expectations and allow yourself to be pleased when your expectations are met or exceeded. This reduces the chance of being let down and gives everyone in the relationship room to breathe and to grow. This also enables you to better manage and optimize your own energy.

7. *Step Away from Abusive Relationships.*

   Do not rely on abusive people for nurture or support. Taking on abuse from anyone takes away your personal power – it is de-energizing and pulls you away from accessing light. Be proactive and recognize when there are abusive people in your life and step away and cancel these relationships. This can be hard, but necessary. Even when these may be family members – learn to love them from a distance. Wish them well and wish them growth.

8. <u>*Create Your Own Family.*</u>

We live in an 'organic' age. Go ahead and create your own family circle from among close and trusted friends, distant relatives, or authority figures. If you do not have a close nurturing biological family, create an extended family. These can be relatives, friends or mentors who give you emotional and spiritual support.

9. <u>*Be Discerning When Choosing Your Friends and Associations.*</u>

Outside of school and work you choose the people who will populate your life 100% of the time. The people you allow or bring into your life circle are a direct reflection of how you feel about yourself. These are some of the most important choices you will make in your journey. You choose your friends. Even when people approach you first, you decide whether to enter a relationship with them. And remember, your enemies also choose you. The people you choose will strongly influence your quality of life. They play a role in how much pain or joy, conflict, or peace you will experience in that relationship. Choose people who have a healthy attitude about themselves as you do. Choose those who are positively motivated, who treat you well and can help you to grow. Choose those with whom you feel safe to be yourself. This is so important in today's world. Respect your circle of life. Pay careful attention to the quality of energy that people bring to their relationships with you, AND to the quality of energy you are putting into those relationships.

Formula 9

CHAPTER SIX

KISSING THE SKY – WORKING WITH UNIVERSAL LAWS

The greatest prosperity in life is not associated with money or even with the worldly things that have no inherent quality but represent a power to buy. Good health, a moderate enjoyment of the necessities of life, a happy and contented mind, a sureness of what will be made manifest on the morrow, a lack of fear regarding the so-called unknown probabilities of life, a rational and understandable attunement with the Consciousness of the Creator and the Spiritual Mind of the Universe, the fortunate ability to make friends and hold them, to spread sunshine and happiness, to find ways and means of helping others (without the use of money or material things)—these are the things that represent the true prosperity of life. A person who has most of these would not abandon them, trade them, exchange them or sell them for all the money, the gold, the jewels or material assets of this Earth.

- H. Spencer Lewis

'Scuse me while I kiss the sky!

- Jimi Hendrick

Purple Haze

The human soul aspires towards spirituality more than to religiosity. Universal laws are spiritual canons that we are innately dependent upon in this aspiration. Universal laws are the foundational principles that govern human conduct, realities, and probabilities within creation and without these laws no manifestations can occur or exist. These laws are ubiquitous in scope, efficacy, and soundness. They are of providence and expressions of the *cosmic energy* and *order* that humanity can discern. Universal laws are authoritative, sovereign, fixed and immutable. As with the universe, these laws are fundamentally constructive and inclined towards growth and expansion - operating in the realm of mind and spirit.

The universal laws of mind and spirit undergird and govern our lives. These indelible laws, like the laws of nature, physics, aerodynamics, and math, irrefutably orchestrate all activity in their relevant plane. And as such, universal laws are always in force and operating. It is prudent and wise to know and live within these laws; for they touch every life equally and cooperate with human free will; they are always at labor whether anyone is aware of this or not - 24/7 and 12 months a year. Knowing, understanding, and working in harmony with these laws is the 9th Key of Formula 9 - and crucial to living a more conscious life.

Although they are quite real, universal laws are overshadowed by the more mundane rules and laws that we abide and follow in our everyday affairs. We are, by and large, blind to the universal laws and how these are infused in every aspect of our conscious existences. Before we can understand and consciously work with universal laws, we must remove the blindfold and open our eyes to see.

When you acknowledge and live in your fullest awareness of universal laws as you do with other natural laws, and when you understand and accept how these laws are active in your life and work with them, you are well on track to raising your consciousness and quality of life. You are in that process. This author asserts that breaking free into a new awareness to accept and live in harmony with universal laws of mind and spirit is tantamount to *"Kissing the sky"*, as Jimi Hendrick belted out in his iconic: *Purple Haze*.

The universal laws of mind and spirit are numerous. They govern how spiritual energy is generated and how it manifests and flows in and through our lives. These represent the foundational rules and mechanics around which sub-atomic energetic vibrations and frequencies resonate. The concepts and tools provided in this book are based on several universal laws. Here are twelve laws that are directly related to enabling you to raise your consciousness, and thereby bringing you closer to the object of your desire. Each law is distinct; however, these laws are linked and flow into one another. Specifically, the Law of Vibration, Law of Manifestation, Law of Attraction and Law of Karma (Cause and Effect) collectively represent the core 'expansive and generative' spiritual laws of the universe which govern personal growth and evolution; and from which all the other laws stem. Through reflection and intention, you can 'know' how these laws of mind and spirit inform, shape, and govern your experiences; and you can understand and witness how these laws operate in the wide world. Learning to work with these laws is a super-effective life skill.

The Law of Change and Evolution

Change and evolution are closely linked. One is the extension of the other. One cannot occur without the other. Like the ever-changing and expanding universe, change is the essential process for all existence, it pushes us to evolve! For humans are in essence angels in becoming. Humankind has achieved amazing feats, mostly in the domain of the hard sciences: medical, engineering, mechanical, aerospace, technology, biochemistry, etc. Yet, humanity still has a huge mountain to climb in terms of its collective evolution to its original state of oneness with the Divine. Change is the 'apparatus' which aids humanity with this ascent.

Change

Things change. The one thing that you can rely on in this life is change. Change is the only constant. Yes, you've heard this before, and it will always ring true. The Law of Change and Evolution is no doubt, the most challenging and frustrating to people. It rams against the way people want to view and conduct their lives. Change uproots and snatches us out of our comfort zones because that is what it is meant to do. The good news is that when you can and do embrace the Law of Change and Evolution, you are on the winning side and have leverage!

Life is dynamic. Seasons come and go; birds migrate; technologies mutate and accelerate; people transform and transition; pop singers become jazz singers, and so on. Change is necessary for growth and betterment; without it, progress is impossible. Change is an instigator and enforcer. At the human level, change spurs one to evolve, to move, to live more fully, to become better. Once a person becomes settled in and comfortable in a situation or routine, something inevitably happens to shake things up. While an unexpected and even unwelcome change can be upsetting or troubling, it is intrinsically moving us forward. Change brings new growth and opportunities to learn and improve. Change is like the wind that blows through the trees, shaking the dead leaves away and creating openings for new buds to sprout forth. In time, the tree becomes stronger with the new green growth.

When you are not growing, the Law of Change and Evolution will bust you out of your routine. It will present you with a task or trial to engage you to stretch in some way. Resisting change intensifies the problems and challenges that may plague you at a given time – bringing about suffering – as in struggling against the currents of a river.

Raising your consciousness means embracing the awareness that change will be your constant companion, and being poised to be flexible, to move and bend and stretch as you must and as a way of life. Expecting and recognizing change when it comes, and trusting change naturally lifts your consciousness.

Evolution

James Moody, the legendary jazz musician said: *"You should grow in some way every day. When I am growing, I give better things."* Evolution is redeeming and elevating the spirit. By evolving one willfully elevates their spirit to its universal original state of love, peace, and oneness with the *Divine.* The imperative to evolve is inherent in all life forms. A rose evolves to be the most beautiful flower; and in its perfection, it has thorns. Like the rose, there is an inborn mechanism to evolve within us; it is self-generating. In our personal evolutions we uncover and render layers upon layers of ourselves. What and who we are 'becoming' requires all of those parts – the petals and the thorns. It is the process that matters most because we never stop evolving!!! Our lives are wedded to the laws that govern the universe, and which sponsor our personal growth and evolution. Everyone shares the impetus to evolve whether they realize it or not - this is what we are here to do. As souls, we incarnate because we desire to evolve spiritually. We are travelers on the earth plane; and life's journey is like a classroom where we learn lessons that help us grow and evolve - to become better, and better, and better. This can be thrilling when we can 'see' and are aware of how this is happening – our evolutionary process, which defies aging! Learning and growing is a conscious choice made from free will. It is important to pay attention to what we are learning in this classroom in the grand course called 'Life'. As long as people continue to ignore the divinity within them in the forms of Divine wisdom, higher faculties and abilities, and not utilize these in all that they do, they will continue to exist at the level of creatures in the animal kingdom. Put more bluntly, when we are not learning and growing, we are in fact, devolving - we are like the 'walking dead'.

Growing your consciousness means learning the lessons from what is going on around you, and from what is happening to you, and applying your 'tools'. We can learn and grow through the pain of our disharmonious acts, our mistakes, and failures, and through our useful deeds and our successes. We can learn something when we are at our worst and when we are shining. It is all evolution and in accordance with the Law of Change and Evolution. And sometimes when it appears that you are not evolving you might be in a subtle reality making progress.

Accumulating power, money and material possessions is not necessarily learning, growing, and evolving. These things decorate your life. When you look back on your journey 5, 10, and 30 years from now, you want to bear witness as to how you progressed and became better, which can be measured emotionally, mentally, socially, and spiritually. When you reflect on your journey, you want to see if you have become smarter, more loving and loved, more giving, better at receiving, or wiser. You want to see if you honed or produced a talent, how many lives you touched in a meaningful way, or if you put something useful into the world.

The key to aligning with the Law of Change and Evolution is to understand and appreciate the lessons life brings to you and applying what you are learning. This law dictates that when you are learning and growing you are closer to the object of your desire – even living it. Life is more interesting and fulfilling. You vibrate at a higher level and are more magnetic – attracting the things that you want and progressing. Your capacity to live consciously in an uncertain world that is ever-changing keeps you in harmony with the Law of Change and Evolution.

The Law of Free Will

Free will is the power to act without the constraints of fate. This applies to 'waking consciousness' and mental competence. As human beings we are all endowed with 'free will'. Free will distinguishes humans from animals as it marks a decisive stage in the evolution of consciousness. It allows humans to take their destinies into their own hands and choose the paths their lives will take. Free will precedes all the decisions and choices one makes, this includes one's thoughts, emotions, intentions, and reactions to life circumstances. A person is always choosing how they are thinking, feeling, and acting. The primary ability and power a person has in his and her life is the 'free will' to choose and decide. When you think about it, everything you thought, felt, or did within the past 24 hours came from a choice that you made. A person is never presented with a situation where she and he cannot or does not choose how they will respond or effect an action; they will always possess the 'free will' to do so. Even when a person may be in a forced situation, she and he uses their free will to determine how to deal with the situation.

Our 'free will' is an indelible part of our 'human package'. Although other factors influence a life to some extent, 'free will' is always there and being exercised. No one does this for us no matter how compelling the situation may be; and with our 'free will' we can mitigate the impact of events and even transcend events entirely.

Free will dignifies us. With 'free will', it is not easy to say that somebody made you do this or do that, or somebody made you mad or even happy. Really, you are fundamentally choosing what you 'will' think, 'will' feel, and how you 'will' act and react all the time, which makes you essentially responsible for your actions and how you show up in the world. Even when it comes to people who feel victimized, feeling victimized stems from the choice to be a victim and powerless. One can give their power away for others to victimize them, and this is a choice made of their own free will.

Your 'locus of control' orientation is an extension of your 'free will'. This means that you use your 'free will' to decide that you 'will' operate from an internal locus of control or from an external one. This realization can be either liberating or a burden depending on the locus of control orientation you choose and how you exert it. An internal locus of control stems from a more empowered sense of free will as opposed to an external locus of control. From this empowered place your awareness of your personal mastery over the events of your life is heightened; you direct your 'free will' more responsibly, and with greater positive impact on your experiences and circumstances.

Free will is an important universal law because it keeps us grounded in the awesome creative power to fashion our experiences to a significant degree. When you are willing and ready to step into a more conscious way of life, making reflection a regular part of it, and minding your locus of control you are riding high with the Law of Free Will.

The Law of Vibration

(Core Expansive/Generative Law)

All is energy. Everything vibrates. The infinite universe operates on the principle of 'vibrational energy'. You are energy vibrating at a distinctive level. The body you inhabit is essentially trillions and trillions of rapidly oscillating atoms and molecules which are broken down into waves and particles - moving at your personal vibrational rate. The vibrational rate of your body is tuned just right to provide a vehicle for your life force. Your thoughts are energy vibrating at a specific rate as well as your emotions. Energy vibrates at different levels - from lower to higher. The higher the rate that energy vibrates, the less dense it becomes. The less dense energy becomes the lighter and freer it is to shift, shape and generate forms of matter and experiences. The energy of your thoughts and emotions are less dense than the energy composing your physical body and are therefore the primary instruments you use to shape your life and experiences. This happens with and without your conscious awareness. Consciousness is energy. And people vibrate at different rates according to their individual levels of consciousness evolution.

In terms of consciousness, the higher the vibration the more evolved you become and more adept at 'willfully' manifesting in the physical and spiritual planes. You want to be mindful of the Law of Vibration by staying aware of the levels at which you are vibrating and how your thoughts and feelings are *affecting* and *influencing* your vibrational levels. Positivity fuels higher vibrations, whereas negativity consequentially fuels lower vibrations. This is the Law. The disciplined practice of reflection helps you to raise your vibration because in this process you allow yourself to see into the nature of things and of your life - to see what is needed and what should be discarded. The more 'stuff' of psyche from lower energies you discard the lighter your consciousness becomes and the higher you vibrate and access light. You get the same result with higher energies you choose to make your own.

The Law of Manifestation

(Core Expansive/Generative Law)

Human beings are perpetually manifesting their reality. The Law of Manifestation is closely interrelated with the Law of Vibration. Manifest means *to be easily apparent to the senses* - to be seen and experienced. The Law of Manifestation refers to the process by which things and experiences come into existence as a direct result of the vibration of our thoughts, emotions, intentions, and expectations. In your life, physical and experiential manifestations begin as an energy unit of thought, emotion or the energy of an idea. These automatically trigger the manifesting process. You are always manifesting - it is intrinsic to being human - with most people manifesting their experiences unconsciously. Going back to the Law of Vibration, the more conscious you are of the levels at which you are vibrating and controlling how you are vibrating, the more consciously you can work with the Law of Manifestation to *manifest* the object of your desire.

With the Law of Manifestation, you have within your consciousness the motive capacity to bring about the object of your desire, hence, to generate your reality. It is like being ambulatory – having strong and healthy legs and being able to move around or steering a car. You have immeasurable creative power within you to manifest - and it costs you nothing. This forceful act simply requires that you make the effort to cultivate it consciously by being aware that it is operating and by fueling it with good quality thoughts, feelings, etc. – good vibrations!

The Law of Attraction

(Core Expansive/Generative Law)

What distinguishes the Law of Attraction from the Law of Manifestation is that while you are always energetically manifesting, you are also attracting to you that which *matches* your thoughts, feelings, and general state of consciousness. This is how three of the 'core expansive and generative laws' work together: The vibration you have is the root or source (material); the manifestation is the process by which the vibration moves or reaches out to attract what matches it. A more colorful analogy is: Your vibration is the *fuel*; how you manifest is the *automotive vehicle*; what you attract is the *destination.* Your strong and consistent thoughts and feelings run through all of these components – the fuel, vehicle and destination, including the *GPS* that guides you there. *Contaminated or poor quality fuel, driving under the influence and a faulty GPS will make it unlikely that you get where want to go.* And vice versa.

With the Law of Attraction, you can only attract those qualities to you that you already possess. Where your attention flows, your energy also goes; and where your energy goes, it returns to you in kind. You attract to you what you are and what you intently focus on whether it is positive or negative. You attract what you think about, whether you desire what you get or not. Your thoughts, beliefs, intentions, and expectations are like powerful magnets that attract situations that agree with them. This makes the Law of Attraction the most potent universal law. This law is at work in your life every day, every hour, every minute, and microsecond. It is highly cooperative. The way it works is analogous to a puppy, anxious to please, wagging its tail waiting for you to throw it a bone for it to run and fetch. The Law of Attraction is always at your beck and call - there for you to give it a thought or belief to fulfill. You must take extra care with what you put into the world through your everyday thoughts, emotions and intentions. The Law of Attraction will always make the picture in your deepest mind come true.

According to the Law of Attraction and the Law of Free Will you control what you think and believe, which makes you responsible for much of what happens to you. This is hard for many people to accept. Working harmoniously with this Law requires a deep intimate knowledge and acquaintance with your thought, belief and feeling patterns and the reality these are generating for you. If you find that these do not serve you, and you are not satisfied with your present reality you can and should change these. You can change your thought, emotional and belief patterns and subsequently, your behaviors to generate a new reality; you have the same power to quash deep-seated thought and belief patterns that have repeatedly attracted to you problems and dissatisfaction by altering their energetic quality and vibration. When a film director becomes dissatisfied with her production, she can *say "Cut, change this script. It's not working here!"* The same applies within the recesses of your mind. With the Law of Attraction ready and at bay to serve you, you can write and launch a fresh new script. Power, money and material possessions are merely props; they are not instruments for learning, growing, and evolving. Real spiritual power is exercising your 'free will' to cultivate different patterns of thinking, feeling, intending, and behaving when the existing patterns you may be projecting are not serving you well.

Again, your strong and enduring thoughts and feelings NEVER occur in a vacuum. The Law of Attraction is fundamentally neutral and will strictly obey the energy of your thoughts, feelings, and intentions, and on whatever you focus on intently and infuse with your consciousness energy. Having the consciousness to positively manage your core thought and feeling vibrations is key to working harmoniously with the Law of Attraction and making it work for you rather than against you. This steadfast Law insures that you will manifest the reality you desire and that you innately feel you deserve - be it a nightmare or paradise.

The Law of Karma

(Core Expansive/Generative Law)

The evolution of consciousness goes hand in hand with karma - the inescapable law of cause and effect. Karma, a basic law that pervades the universe, is that all beings are the rightful owners of their deeds. All human thought, speech and actions are charged with some degree of mental, emotional, or spiritual 'affect' - baggage. What you put out you get back. The Law of Karma is the way of the universe to maintain balance and harmony. According to this law there is no such thing as 'chance'. Chance is merely a term indicating that a cause exists but is not perceived or recognized. Disharmonious deeds must be balanced at some point in each human experience to achieve optimal growth. As we are using free will to manifest and attract, we are also destined to grow and evolve in the process. The Law of Karma requires a *'responsibility'* in the way we vibrate, manifest, and attract. We are not here to occupy a space on the planet, but to learn and grow and evolve towards our highest capacities. This is played out in the arena of our deeds and the lessons we learn along the way. One must always be mindful of the quality of what they put into the world in terms of thoughts, feelings, and deeds. Because what they put into the world comes back to that person and is measured and counted towards their level of growth and evolution in their journey. This is like pouring water into a well; sooner or later one must drink from that well. Therefore, it is prudent to be mindful of the quality of water one places into the well. So goes the Law of Karma.

The natural impulse of the energies of the universe is to constantly expand; because we are composed of the same 'star stuff' of the universe we are also here to expand our being. We grow and evolve through karma.

Relationships are where we generate most of our karma - for good and bad; and relationships are where the Law of Karma or 'cause and effect' is keenly operative. This is why some relationships we have are more charged than others. We subconsciously seek and gravitate to those who have a particular karmic configuration that our souls need to help us work out some karma or to learn a specific lesson. It is in these 'karmic' relationships where there is a major growth imperative for one or both parties.

According to the Law of Karma, you are always exactly where you are supposed to be and living exactly the life meant for you to live to learn 'your' lessons. You will continue to attract and have certain experiences and circumstances until you learn the lesson inherent in that particular experience. Through reflection and growing your consciousness you can discover the lessons you are here to learn; and you can witness how you are learning and growing from these lessons. When you have learned and integrated that learning into your life, you can minimize and even move past karmic lessons and beyond the negative karma that generated those disharmonious experiences. Reflection, optimizing your energy and light and being mindful of the kinds of relationships you engage builds your capacity to manage karma for the better as you continue to learn and grow. With your karma in balance you vibrate at a higher level and are more magnetic – attracting experiences that can make your life more satisfying and interesting.

The Law of Abundance

Most people are too steeped and distracted with pain and suffering to know that life pulsates with beauty, love, joy, and pleasure. Life in essence, is to be lived fully and prosperously. The earthly experience is an extension and part of an expansive, creative, and generative universe. Life is truly abundant as evidenced in nature. Luxury, comfort, enjoyment, leisure, and the generosity from others are important along with work, creativity or making a positive contribution to humanity and life on the planet. These and money are forms of wealth – and wealth is good. The human spirit needs pampering; this adds to life and helps to evolve consciousness and our capacity to appreciate the delights that life has to offer. You have within you the wherewithal to make your earthly incarnation a paradise; and you can choose to accept that this is your divine birthright.

The universe is abundantly generous – not scarce or stingy. There is more than enough of what is 'good' to go around. Although most of the people populating our planet view it as a universe of scarcity - as reflected in their thought and belief patterns. We humans predominately give reign to our fears and 'scarcity consciousness' in this experience, which cloud the treasures and pleasures that are inherit in the lived experience. Raising your consciousness is to know this; and containing and shedding your fears and worries and doubts - like becoming a child again, who is pure in faith, anticipation, and the assurance that she and he are safe and well provided for. You were meant to have your needs and wants met, and the Law of Abundance operates to help make this a reality.

The universe is in a perpetual process of providing and balancing - inclined to create and generate. It will respond and provide you with what you are focusing on intently. The Law of Abundance is closely aligned with the 'core expansive/generative laws' that meet you where you are and fills the orders you place with your thoughts, feelings, beliefs, and expectations – *and this Law is set up to do this ten times over!* It is poised to fulfill the object of your desire.

The Law of Abundance builds on what you already have and what you are already doing. It multiplies! It is triggered into action by your strong desires. To positively activate the Law of Abundance you must tear down the wall of limiting thoughts, beliefs, expectations and fears that block life's gifts for you. Through reflection you can refine your thought processes to be more positively energized and filled with light; you can clarify your expectations and what it is that you desire and why. With this, you can better vibrate harmoniously with the Law of Abundance.

Here is an example of how this works. *I was shopping in a small specialty store for cosmetics. From the moment I entered the store the woman manager approached and began lamenting to me her frustration about an incident, whereby a customer brought in a lot of drama and treated her harshly - with yelling and threatening her. She was all in my ears with this; clearly using this opportunity with me to vent. And then her tirade morphed into the story of her life about the many abuses and injustices she suffered from people and the 'system', etc., when all she wanted was love and respect. Her energy was defiant, hard, and fierce. Through this I could see that she was a decent person, basically who was hurt, and had been consumed with fighting and fending off attacks to protect herself from more harm. But her desires did not match the 'energy' that she was putting out. She treated me quite well; she just wanted me to listen to her stories and frustrations. I went into the same store a week later and she was there, presenting me with a new line of frustrations about rude customers and a more recent worse scenario of a near physical altercation and police involvement. It was apparent that the woman was anguishing and wanted to be treated with kindness and respect; yet she was manifesting the opposite and in spades! The 'abundant' universe was simply granting her what she was intently focusing on through her thought processes and charged emotional energy, and sadly, gave her a larger dose of it too!*

Know that the Law of Abundance is hyperactive and there to provide you with what you concentrate on – in big amounts. If you fail at something, be mindful not to beat up on yourself and sink into negativity, despair and pessimism because the Law will respond by matching your thoughts and mood with more of the same – maybe much more. If the disappointment or hurt is too much and you must have a 'pity party', put a time limit on it and get back on track. Wallowing can make things worse. Learn to feed yourself and maintain higher and positive thoughts at all costs. When you fail or are not at your best, try to get into the habit of fueling yourself with healthy thoughts; forgive yourself and let yourself know and feel that you are always working with the best that you have at a given time. Knowing and focusing positively on the object of your desire keeps the channels clear. Gratitude excites and ignites the Law of Abundance as well as stretching your innate capacity to receive.

The Law of Gratitude

One of the most important things a person can say is *"Thank you"*. These two simple words, expressed with sincerity and regularity have immense power. The Law of Gratitude requires one to refrain from taking things for granted - this includes one's blessings and tribulations. The Law of Gratitude works in our day-to-day life. It is the gateway to abundance.

An ongoing 'attitude of gratitude' makes everything it touches shine, sparkle and glow. Being in gratitude activates an energetic magnetism that draws more to you. The more you give by expressing gratitude, the more you can receive. Gratitude unlocks and unblocks; it keeps a positive flow of energy going from and coming to you. Gratitude is a potent antidote for much of what troubles, plagues and tries us in life as well as helps us to grow our consciousness and access light. The energy of 'gratitude' is like a magic wand that instantaneously shifts a mood, a bad feeling, even a dreadful situation. Gratitude chases away fear. Exuding an attitude of gratitude makes it difficult for negativity and lower energies to penetrate your zone of psyche. It shields you from worry, distress and hopelessness; it fosters good health and enhances your well-being, and bursts open the doors of possibility. Expressing gratitude automatically boosts your energetic vibration levels, which in turn, increases your ability to manifest with greater quality. For all of these things and more, because 'gratitude' energy is so pure, it cannot do otherwise! This is the Law.

Working with the Law of Gratitude is as simple as entertaining a random 'affirmative' thought or a feeling. It means acknowledging that there is always something to be grateful for. In your private mind you can say a simple *Thank you"* for a sunny day, for getting out of bed in the morning, a baby's bright smile at you, or for a lesson learned. The occasions to express gratitude are ALL around you ALL the time.

The Law of Detachment

Life is not always pleasant and wonderful. We are privileged to experience moments of joy, splendor, and happiness in our journeys. However, life brings pain, turmoil, challenges, and adversity. There is the perpetual dance of the positive and negative. It is a universal law that we are energetically bound to that which we strongly resist. The Universal Law of Detachment is based on energetic principles as are the other laws. According to the Law, the energy that we put into resisting something - be it a person or situation, will continue to attract that person or situation to us - it will cling to us. As in the Law of Attraction that 'like will attract like', the Law of Detachment similarly holds that you are always attracting the things to you that match your energetic vibrations. However, in this law you will attract the things you abhor and detest - and especially these. In many cases in life, it is our resistance to something that causes our suffering - which are usually the things that are not working in our lives: Relationship problems, loss, loneliness, economic hardships, illness, and desires that go unfulfilled, etc. Ironically, we tend to have strong energetic 'charges' around these kinds of things – the things we don't want, that make us unhappy, and that we vehemently complain about; and it is the 'charge' around it that acts as a powerful magnet or 'glue' that makes those 'things' stick to us.

What you complain about, you claim. Pushing against situations that you do not like or want will only bind you to them. Working in alignment with this Law means to think and speak on what you 'want' rather than on what you don't want. This is necessary even when you find yourself consumed and right in the middle of intense negative and unsatisfying circumstances, maybe even being righteously teed off. Heightened consciousness means knowing not to resist the things you don't want or that do not make you happy and rather to accept these as facets of your life, and perhaps connected to lessons you need to learn. It is to regard these 'things' as energy or forces that are moving in and through your life. These may be in your life for a reason and are there to play a role in your evolutionary process. Learning the lessons meant for you makes it easier to detach and eventually become released from certain persons or kinds of experiences. With your conscious 'detachment', problems and issues can behave like an energy stream that filters through your life. Like smoke. This can better happen when you are involved but detached and not resisting these nagging 'things' in terms of how you think, feel or speak about them. Hence, rather than resisting, acknowledging, and recognizing something for what it is diffuses its energy and impact in your life. This is the Law of Detachment. Working with this Law means to change what you can, while having the presence and wisdom to accept some unalterable situations as they are. In this way you will preserve your time, and mental and physical energies to affect the things that you can. From this attitude of acceptance and non-resistance comes the kind of 'involved detachment' that enables you to enjoy the positives in your life while allowing the negatives to flow out and away - affecting you less. Clarity of your locus of control helps to sustain an attitude of detachment when you are troubled or challenged.

Another aspect of the Law of Detachment is 'letting go'. This can be hard at times. When you let go of things, persons or situations when you need to and without a 'charge' attached to it, you make space for something of equal or greater consequence to come through. For the universe unerringly seeks to fill a void.

The Law of Unconditional Love

"Love is all there is." That is a famous quote coined by author Emily Dickinson many years ago. There is deep truth and staying power in what she said. Beyond the distractions of materialism and the facade of everyday life, there is love. The real spiritual meaning and force of love that undergirds every life goes unnoticed when people are distracted and blinded under the veneer of mundane living. Piercing through that is an act of consciousness-raising; and in doing so more can be realized; we can see better - that love births the good. And I would take what Dickinson said further to attest that 'love is all that we have'.

Classical philosophers and theologians held the idea that: *"The whole of creation was the result of Divine Love and that it was by the expansion of this Love that the universe, nature and humanity came into existence."* The union of matter with consciousness is really a 'love story'. Love is a force that underlies all that was, is and will be. There is no widely held definition of love; the modern, although incomplete definition of love is: *'The inclination to want the good of another besides oneself'*. We are creations of love and from that are meant to be vehicles of love. En masse we have diverted away from this primary force and become swooned into fear which makes reconnecting with the 'force of love' one of humanity's noblest goals. Love is a quality of energy in one of its highest forms. Love is pure, positive, and elevated energy. Love is a composite of seeking the *good*, of raising the *good*, of acknowledging and sharing the *good*; it is being the *good* and shining the *good* onto the world; it is nurturing and allowing the *good*. There are many kinds of love; from parental, to romantic, to self-love and cosmic love *(love of God, Divinity and good)*. Compassion, empathy and kindness are tenets of love; they are virtues that energetically vibrate on higher frequencies than other emotions and attitudes such as anger, guilt, cynicism, resentment, and shame. Love does not possess, nor can it be contained. It is experienced as energy that we give and receive, and as a key ingredient for our well-being. Humans instinctively know love when it is experienced, as love is a basic human need as essential as food and water and air. It is practically impossible to survive without love.

As a force, 'love' is primary in the laws of mind and spirit, which is experienced and expressed in emotional and mental states. Where love is present it can cause people and circumstances to radiate at a higher level - making it hard for negativity and lower energies to seep in or thrive. With the expression of unconditional love, one naturally rises above hate and transcends fear because love is the opposite of fear. The Law holds that love and hate/fear energies cannot occupy the same space; and that the strong presence of 'love' will ultimately impart a balance, truce, or truth into a situation. The Law of Unconditional Love is void of judgment and expectations of others. With the Law of Unconditional Love, one does not seek to change, but respects the other's sojourn in life without trying to control or interfere. And while we realistically cannot love everyone, it is a universal imperative to hate no one.

Within each person the Law of Unconditional Love is also operating. 'Knowing Thyself" is an act of self-love. Loving others begins with love for oneself. This is reflected by applying the principles of non-judgement, kindness, compassion and empathy towards oneself and having realistic expectations for oneself – the same things that we do for others. It is unashamedly using every opportunity that one can to lift and support oneself and to hold oneself in high esteem. As an increasingly 'conscious' person, the 'force' of love becomes a tool and an ally to fortify your powers of manifestation. When you are consciously manifesting at a high energy level in your relationships with others and yourself you are aligned with the Law of Unconditional Love. Collectively, the energy of love connects us stronger than other forces. Unconditional love that is deep, true and selfless enough can alter the future; it can prevent wars and stop a plague. It is the one note of the human symphony that can make impossible humanity's self-destruction and keep the world whole.

The Law of Connection and One

Everything and everyone are imbued with the universal influx of cosmic consciousness. The Law of Connection and One governs and is highly operating in all human relationships. Every person is connected at the level of 'collective consciousness'. Here, I illustrate this point. *While on a train ride from Aschaffenburg Germany to Berlin, a man seated across the aisle from my son kept rudely interjecting into my son's business. He was asking if my son was sure that he was seated in the right section (which cost more) insinuating that my son was doing something wrong, and he was making intrusive comments about what my son and his friend were taking out of their backpacks. My son was annoyed, but more tired and sleepy and did not want to react to engage in conflict with the man. In his mind he told himself that if the man said anything else to him he was going to say to him: "Ist dir langweilig?" – meaning, are you bored? The man went on to bug the woman who was seated in a row nearby in the same manner and telling her that his name was Christian. The woman's little son, of about 6 years old was seated with her, quietly watching a movie on his computer. As the man continued to annoy his mother, the boy suddenly, turned to Christian and asked: "Ist dir langweilig Christian?"* The little boy was 'tapped in' to my son's vibe and thinking and he did the thing for my son. There are several spiritual layers to what happened here, for the 'veil' between my son's and the boy's consciousnesses was very thin. The main thing is that it demonstrated how we are connected; and when episodes such as this occur, it is merely, *life being normal.*

The overt separations between and among us that we acknowledge and wrap our lives around are at best secondary; at the levels of consciousness these are null and void.

We are all linked with and feed into the ONE and are all part of the gestalt energy of the universe. Keeping with the nature of this universal energy, which is to expand and generate, we are here to move the collective energy forward – to generate higher vibrations of energy for us all. We do this by learning and growing with and through one another as we share this earth environment. We increase the vibrational levels both individually and collectively by honoring our spiritual connection. Because we are part of 'one', what we think, feel, say, and do affects other souls - both near and far. There exists a natural kinship among everyone regarding their attitudes, actions, and experiences, even in our innermost thoughts and desires, as in my son's experience with the little boy on the train. Really, one person's joy or misery affects multitudes of others, at some level. What we do to another person and to the earth we are doing to ourselves and everyone else.

The Law of Connection and One mandates that we acknowledge ourselves as a 'member of the world'. Your personal growth and development are inevitably linked to the people who cross your path throughout your life. There is very little that you can or cannot do without links to other people. It is through connections with others that opportunities come to you, and through which you achieve your goals. And truth be told, the 'world wide web' is making this reality more manifest. In accordance with the Law of Connection and One your relationship with the world is just as important as your relationship to your 'self'. The more you connect your goals to a larger purpose, the more meaning you will have in your life, and the richer this experience becomes for you. Raising your personal vibration by living 'right' within yourself and among others is the single greatest contribution you can make to the evolution of humankind on the planet.

The Law of Divine Order

The preceding laws of the universe regulate to achieve order and natural balance. There is divine order in what seems to be a chaotic universe. All is as it should be to prompt us to evolve individually and collectively – we are exactly where we should be individually and collectively, regardless of how awful and disconcerting it may look and seem. With the Law of Divine Order, there are no accidents. All is in order, even within chaos. This order is a reflection of who we are, how far we've come, and which points us to where we need to go. The synchronicities, magical moments, and phenomenal coincidences you may experience from time to time are windows into the perfection and divine order of the universe. These are direct answers to what you have already been wondering or intending – confirmations of your powers of manifestation; they are reminders from the universe that it is alive, present and moving in our lives. I call these *'cosmic kisses'*. The order in the universe assures that you always have the opportunities and experiences you need to learn, grow, evolve and to work through karma. And *'As above, so below'*. The law implies that what happens at the individual level also occurs at the level of the whole of humanity. The order in the universe will obey the collective thoughts, words, and deeds of humans to generate the larger, macro environment for us all. When enough human souls vibrate their energy upon such things as peace, the divine order in the universe will respond to reflect peace and less fear in the world.

* * *

These perfect laws of the universe are essential tools and partners in your journey. Together these laws represent the natural 'justice' of the universe which seeks to vouchsafe your birthright to personal/spiritual unfolding and evolution. Take time to give thought to the grandeur of the universe.

CHAPTER SEVEN

THE UNIVERSITY
OF YOU

*What we fear doing most is usually
what we most need to do.*
- Ralph Waldo Emerson

*People don't grow by accident they grow
by design. Design yourself, design your future.
Success never just happens.*
- Anonymous

*There will be no butterflies if life does not go through
long and silent metamorphosis.*
- Rubem Alves

At *'YOUniversity'* there is dynamic learning and scholarship. The core curriculum is *Lifelong Learning and Growth*. There is no tuition, no textbooks, no prerequisites, time limits, exams, or GPA to be had. You learn at your own pace and level. YOU are the teacher and the student. The self-guided courses are culled from your everyday life affairs, from your relationships, from who you are, want to be and are becoming. The classroom and lab work are in the corridors of your consciousness through which you graduate to ever higher degrees.

This Sacred Journey

Living fully in today's world requires the personal mastery which comes from cultivating and elevating one's consciousness. We are besieged on a regular basis with events and impressions that require us to make choices and decisions. We make hundreds of choices and decisions every day from major to slight - from deciding what kind of drink we will have in the morning, to how to deal with the way someone spoke to us, to whether to respond to an invitation to attend an event that is entirely new for us. We largely make these choices and decisions automatically without much forethought simply because there is so much coming at us. And the rate and volume of data, information, and impressions are accelerating and increasing. Because today's world is spinning faster, and with mounting distractions, deadlines, news, connections with people, and with rapid technologies generating more of the same, we cannot help but to be on automatic in our decisions and choices. With the rush and push of the world our choices are usually made to be efficient rather than effective, which makes our decisions uninformed and 'knee-jerk', for the most part. We do not usually have the time to stop and step back to take it all in and to go inside and reflect, or to consult with the *subjective reality* that is always operating and at the heart of everything that is happening to us externally.

This is the age of responsibility. Despite the pull of the raging activities in this world, you can set your own pace and write your own script. This is your sacred journey – to sift through and navigate this earthy plane to become the person you were meant to be. Despite the trials and tumult in the world, and what you see and what is happening around you and to you, YOU are journeying towards your fullest potential. Your journey does not stop or wait - it requires your constant and utmost focus and care. Life is the most precious gift granted to human beings - it is the stage for our spiritual evolution and the laboratory in which we can manifest the desires of our heart. Part of the journey is asking yourself: *"How am I going to navigate my way to 'myself' and in the world amid the activity, problems, distractions, and the conditioning and programming?"*

You Are the Cause

At a dinner gathering in Berlin, I shared the table with several 24–29-year-old adults who were in rapt discussion on the state of the world. Everyone was quite up to date on the events in the Middle East, the ongoing conflicts and warring factions among nations, the entrenched corruptions in politics and world leadership, the refugee crises, climate changes, and more. Although informed, the group did not seem to have an opinion one way or another about those events. So, I posed an obvious question: "How do you feel about what is happening in the world?" Long silence. And then: "I feel helpless," which seemed to be the unanimous sentiment at the table. The group did not have an answer to the troubles in the world. Although they were keenly aware of the problems, and did not like what they saw, they felt powerless that they could not do anything about it. What was also telling about the conversation was their consensus that they *could not get their heads around why things were "So fucked up"*, and asking, *"Why do things have to be this way?"* The mentality behind the happenings in the world just went against their grain. Understandably, what could one person really do when it seemed that the game afoot was beyond reach, in the hands of *others?* Seems the dye had been cast with things locked in, tightly wound and on a roll, and it had been that way for a long time!

I find that there is a temptation to become cynical among adults of the modern generations, especially when they behold the world as it is. This is understandable. Especially in a world that seems to be smirking at you, but and while needing what you have to give. Yet, cynicism, apathy and hopelessness can be a toxic cocktail that does the world no good, nor the individual assuming this psychological stance. Cynicism and apathy can lead one to believe that there is no point – that *"There is nothing I can do, I'm just one person, and it won't make a difference anyway."* The truth is that everyone and anyone can impact the state of things. The world today needs people to get meaningfully involved. This does not necessarily require demonstrating in the streets, or taking on a lot of activities, or even leading people - it can. However, getting involved to effect positive change in today's world is as simple as putting a positively energized and elevated consciousness into the world. This is possible because consciousness is what creates the world. The world today is a direct reflection of humanity's collective consciousness which stems from one person.

The world is rife with problems, chaos, conflict, and blistering wrongs starving for resolution, and where distrust has become a weapon of choice. At the same time there is felicity, progress, triumph, and *spirit* that can be harvested. People from all walks of life – from humble to noble beginnings have made contributions of all kinds which made a difference in the world to advance humankind – still do. Historically, any change for the better and progress in the world began with one person. The new directions that the world is desperate for now can start with you.

Every person has a role to play. The way we live affects everyone on the planet. Every person is here for a reason, whether that person is a graduate from Harvard, Yale, or a community college; whether they are an up-and-coming stockbroker on Wall Street, a demure young Saudi woman about to undertake her education, or a homeless young man roaming the night streets of Kenya. You are here for a reason. You have a purpose and a role to play. Your life has intrinsic value. You are part of the human condition and community, and your essence, talents and contributions are essential towards the betterment of all.

Each one of us is born with a gift - something that defines and distinguishes us from the crowd. However, most of us never tap our true nature or uncover our gifts. This is because most of us do not know the fundamental 'laws', nor have the tools to apply in life - something that our educational nor social systems, even family systems do not inculcate in us. We, for the most part, enter young and adult life unequipped to meet the world in the best possible way and in the way in which we were meant to know it. This can be corrected, beginning with raising our consciousness. You are already 'here', having come this far in this book, which means that you have stepped towards making that commitment.

Appropriately stated in *Transition Now* by Cori, Carroll and Lewis: *"When any human being begins to examine themselves, it creates energy. This real-time effort attributes to how humans create light on the planet."*

Personal mastery begins with self-knowledge and transforming aspects of yourself that work against your highest good. When you transform yourself, you can better effect positive change in the world.

Here is a pertinent story: *One of my graduating Saudi students came to me to share her interest to be the keynote speaker of the university graduation ceremony. She asked me to recommend her to the graduation committee. Although Hala was bright and an A+ student, she also came across as entitled, cocky and behaving as if she was above the rules. I was reluctant to immediately say that I would promote her name, and instead asked her if she could first take some constructive feedback. Without hesitation she said "Yes". So, I told her about the image she had been presenting and how she was perceived by others and even myself, and that it was important that she be a good role model for other graduating students. She admitted that this was hard for her to hear, but in the same sentence asked me what she could do to change that part of herself - saying that it was not her intention to be that way and the feedback from me came as a surprise to her. This was the 'blind spot' part of herself that she was not aware of (Johari Window). I gave her some advice on how to change that image of herself and because I was so impressed with how she responded to the feedback and stepped into her growth process, I told her that I would advance her name to the graduation committee. Weeks leading up to the graduation ceremony, I observed Hala as a different person. She took the lesson to heart and worked to shift from within. In the moments before I gave Hala that feedback, she was smug with the assumption that I would automatically help her; and when I gave her the hard feedback instead, she immediately switched into: 'How can I change to improve myself' mode. This showed courage, humility, and character - of someone willing to commit to her growth and betterment. Days later, she came and thanked me for the feedback saying: "In my culture the person you remember most is the one who tells you the hard things you need to hear." Hala was elected to be the graduation Keynote speaker, and before hundreds of her peers she gave a moving motivational speech filled with respect for her peers - making reference to her recent lesson and growth.*

113

Hala accepted seeing herself as the *cause*. Changing the world for the better really begins with YOU. This is your world. There is no cause to be overwhelmed or discouraged by what is in place or seems to be permanent. You can impact the world. When your purpose aligns with the divine plan for humankind you become its instrument – you partner with the *Divine* and access your greater personal power.

The University of YOU is an alternative course of learning about *you* and the unique force you represent in this resplendent dynamic world. It is diving deeply into your personal psyche, understanding your inner life and what shapes and influences it. It is divining your power to master this inner terrain for your highest good and the good of the whole.

False Evidence Appearing Real

The Fear Program

Fear is the raider; it is the interloper. Fear is a formidable opposition to positive change anywhere, anytime, and anyhow. Fear is the progenitor of the woes that have ravaged humankind for centuries. The world revolves around fear. We are weaned on fear. It is a drug. The ignorance, sadness, conflict, strife, and entrenchments of corruption in the world are the spawn of fear. The earthly plane is dense, and ancestral fear lives and thrives in this density. Within the human psyche, fear is ego-based – trying to push the ego to wield control in a dense world where it ultimately cannot.

Fear is programmed into us as part of our socialization process from childhood into adulthood. Fear is a motivator and a disciplinarian; media, press and advertisers fuel fear to prompt people to consume; employers apply fear to enforce obedience and performance in workplaces. Social and traditional religious institutions pump fear into our psyches. The tendency in the world to over-rationalize is based on fear. The distrust of the inner subconscious world is based on fear. Over-materializing is fear-based. The abject identification with the objective world is modeled on fear. Fear, along with conformity are serious drainers of creative energy.

The toxin of fear consumes and infects our lives, and it takes on many forms. Some forms of fear are:

1. *Fear of life.* Fear of success, failure, closeness and intimacy.

2. *Fear of persecution.* Fear of repercussions if one does not think, believe, or act in a prescribed way that is expected and imposed on us by others.

3. *Fear of being truthful and authentic.* Which stems from fear of not having your needs met if you do not conform - believing that being truthful will deprive you of something or will annihilate you.

4. *Fear of being victimized.* This is helplessness, which is really fear of oneself and one's personal power.

5. *Fear for security and protection.* This is fear that one is not safe, and that one's needs will not be met – that there is never enough to go around – whatever that might be.

6. *Fear that one is defective or inadequate and that others will find this out.* This is guilt and self-shaming.

7. *Fear of the unknown.* Fear of differences and what one does not understand.

8. *Fear of abundance.* A scarcity consciousness which believes that our moments of joy are inevitably short-lived, and that something will surely eventually go wrong. This is also the fear of actually having one's needs met.

9. *Fear of death and annihilation.* Which speaks for itself.

The 'fear program' has us worrying, doubting and holding back more than we should. Overdosing on fear reduces one's access to light. Overdosing on fear distorts the human psyche and opens the floodgates for lower energies, negative emotions and thought habits such as jealously, greed, cynicism, pettiness, hatred, and aggression to come in.

The ego is the aspect of the human personality from which fear is projected; the ego is not the 'fear'; however it gives fear safe harbor. From there, the 'fear' thinks it is in control and seeks to express itself, give advice and draw attention to itself. When the ego allows fear free reign this way it is "**Edging God Out**".

There are fear-based expressions which cannot be expressed from a higher consciousness; these are rather traits that edge their way into one's life through the ego. These are:

1. Anger and rage

2. Competitiveness

3. Insecurity

4. A victim mentality

5. Self-doubt and low self-esteem

6. Selfishness

7. Envy

8. Extreme Anxiety, excessive worrying, over-reacting

9. Impatience

10. A judgmental mentality

No one is perfect. Growing your consciousness is not seeking perfection. Not only is this not possible, but it is not an ideal way of 'being' if you are to experience the fullness of learning and evolving. *Fear cannot save us.* The world will never achieve utopia. When the world gets scary and the affairs of your life seem out of control, it is prudent to stay aware and centered with what you can and do control, which is the quality of your thoughts and emotions, and an awareness of how these forms and traits of fear show up and try to take over your ego. This is also understanding that fear is a construct of the physical plane as *False Evidence Appearing Real.*

The Tyranny of 'Monkey Mind'

'Monkey mind' is the aspect of the ego that is hyper reactive. 'Monkey mind' is the product of the ego, which gets exacerbated by fear when not checked. Monkey mind is also *False Evidence Appearing Real.* Monkey mind goes into automatic to salvage evidence and justifications for the fantasies it wants you to entertain. It can generate obstacles, trip you up and drive you to extremes. This impulse of the ego is always going to be there. It is an aspect of our cultural rational and pragmatic programming - going overboard.

According to Maria Nemeth in *The Energy of Money,* here are some symptoms of 'monkey mind', which I have embellished upon.

1. Being unnecessarily vague.
2. Obsessing on the past and future.
3. Being defensive as a default behavior pattern.
4. Taking things personally when these are not.
5. Feeling easily resigned.
6. Making hesitant commitments.
7. Habitually making excuses for one's faults and errors.
8. Habitual indecisive thinking.
9. Being paranoid.
10. Making unwarranted comparisons.
11. Knee-jerk rationalizing.
12. Deflecting serious concerns with jokes.

13. Being a self-proclaimed martyr.

14. Petulance and cantankerousness.

15. Impulsiveness, rashness.

16. Over concern with what people think/say about you.

17. Small-mindedness/pettiness. Overemphasis on small stuff.

'Monkey mind' as unchecked fear chips away at your evolving state of consciousness. It blocks your energy flow and dims the light. The one clear way to manage 'monkey mind' is first to be aware that it is there and *'doing its thing'* as it were, or as I prefer to say: 'Monkeying around' in the mind. In your awareness you can manage it by challenging the thoughts and impulses that 'monkey mind' is trying to project and 'cancel' these; you can put a new thought or idea in its place that tells a better story. This awareness can be a simple process of flipping the switch from 'monkey mind' mischief (OFF) to engaging the light (ON).

Fear has its upside in some situations, which is that it helps to protect us, making us alert to real danger and threats; warning us and giving us courage to prepare and deal with these. It signals us to be cautious and careful. This is natural fear, much as the creatures of the earth are naturally afraid and instantly flee. The downside of fear outweighs the positives in that it seeks to be the one all-around answer and approach to any and everything, whether it is necessary or not, and where it is more detrimental than useful. Unlike the earth creatures, us humans can transcend fear because we have a distinct 'consciousness' and free will. We can discern and mitigate fear, we can thwart its rule in our lives. Internalizing an acute awareness and understanding of fear is a strong thing to do and enables one to steer clear of fear's antics.

Abundance Consciousness and Scarcity Consciousness

Abundance and scarcity are two fundamental ways that people view and approach life; these are aspects of consciousness. From an abundance consciousness a person believes that there is enough for them, and they will find or attract what they need and deserve; there is always plenty to go around. When one subscribes to a scarcity consciousness, they do not believe that there is enough for their needs to be met, and that they are forever in situations where they lack or cannot have the things they want, and from which they feel they cannot extricate themselves. Scarcity and abundance consciousnesses do not necessarily apply exclusively to material things, but also to qualities such as attention, love, support, and respect. The degree to which we operate from either abundance or scarcity consciousness comes largely from childhood upbringing, which stems from the kinds of values that were pervasive in the family unit and which became instilled within a person as an impressionable child. This also comes from socialization; again, which for the most part, is *fear-based,* with scarcity consciousness being a form of fear.

There are people prone to see the glass as half full and those who are prone to see the glass as half empty. Abundance and scarcity consciousnesses pervade all aspects of our lives; these stances of psyche are more apparent and easily assessed when it comes to problems and challenges. To better know and understand which consciousness you subscribe to you can reflect on how you view and approach your problems, challenges, and life in general. This can reveal the extent to which you are a problem-solver or victimized by circumstances. For example, the person who sees the glass as half full is likely a problem solver and operates from an abundance consciousness; whereas the person who typically sees the glass as half empty tends to feel victimized and powerless in the face of problems and challenges and has a scarcity consciousness. An abundance consciousness opens and enlarges the channels - enabling the person to receive insights and ideas on how to approach matters, they can see possibilities in problems and challenges, they anticipate success; whereas a scarcity consciousness keeps the person stuck and circling around and around that which is not working; they see a wall with no possibilities, and intractable problems, they expect defeat. Abundance consciousness keeps the lights on so to speak, while projecting higher vibrations of energy into the problem situation; whereas scarcity consciousness defuses the light and stagnates the energy around the issue.

Abundance consciousness stems from an internal locus of control, whereas scarcity consciousness tends to be an outgrowth of an overly external locus of control orientation. Following are specific examples of both aspects of consciousness. Understanding these differences and intelligently acting accordingly can make an effective shift in your life experiences. Like internal and external loci of control this is not an either/or dynamic; a person can exhibit most or all of either set of aspects, and some degree of the opposite set of aspects.

With an abundance consciousness one has a sense of gratitude; they are curious lifelong learners who study, research and 'act' to increase their knowledge; they freely share information; they embrace change and are proactive, forgiving and non-judgmental; they accept responsibility for the outcomes of their decisions and choices; they set goals and want others to also succeed; they acknowledge the successes of others - giving credit where it is due. This person usually emanates an aura of 'joie de vie'.

An individual with a scarcity consciousness has a sense of entitlement; they do not engage their mind to learn and expand; they horde information and the energies of others; they fear change; they are reactive and generally do not plan or set goals; they criticize and blame others for their own limitations and failures and hold grudges; they do not acknowledge the successes of others and may secretly want the other person to fail. With this person, manipulation is a skill, and they usually exude anger or rage.

Abundance and scarcity consciousnesses are governed by the universal laws of Attraction, Manifestation, Free will, Vibration and naturally, the Law of Abundance. These laws work together to bring you what you are focusing on, whether it is from a place of abundance or scarcity.

The Consciousness You Keep

Because we are spiritually and cosmically connected, a single ripple of individual consciousness makes a statement and generates an impression in the entire world plane. Anger, fear, jealousy, greed and the like, even ignorance, stemming from individual consciousnesses have shaped much of our human experience. At this juncture in humans' presence on the planet, we have chosen fear and scarcity over abundance; this is reflected in our collective past and present.

Transform We Must

Einstein stated that "*Insanity is trying to solve a problem with the same consciousness that created it.*" And he was right! Because humanity no doubt, is in need of a dramatic shift in consciousness, know this:

1. The life you live is unerringly generated by your present state of consciousness.
2. Your individual consciousness contributes to humans' collective consciousness in the world.
3. The state of the world is a manifestation of humans' collective consciousness.

Consciousness creates the world. Every note of consciousness impacts the world – either actively or passively. You are impacting the world even now by reading this book. In the University of YOU lies the potential to recreate yourself, your reality, and to help recreate the world. Minding the consciousness we keep is a primary responsibility for all of us to carry out in our sacred journeys. This is our collective mission.

The consciousness you keep as an individual is indelibly reflected in the world today. This reality cannot be over-stated. However, the way that we have been systemically socially programmed stifles our growth and evolution as a species. Logically, if we were to heed Einstein's postulation, individual and collective problems can best be solved as we undergo transformations in our individual and collective psyches. This we must do

121

because we have been programmed and impacted in ways that are not in tandem with our spiritual essence as human beings.

One's individual consciousness was at its purest when one was a young child of about 5-6. It was devoid of negative programming and fear. That consciousness did not have the emotions or thought patterns which may have hardened and accumulated over the years of growing into adulthood. Childhood wounds, the lack of self-awareness in adult life along with fear-based programming generates a plague of problems and obstacles. It is not possible to undo this conditioning overnight; yet this challenge does not absolve one from tending to their growth and evolution as best as they can. Likewise, the nurture and positive conditioning one may have received as a child remains infused within them and gives them a strong foundation to work from; yet 'fear' will still be a factor in their adult lives. In either case a person can never get back to the purer state of consciousness they had as a little child. However, whatever the nature of one's upbringing, one can adopt ways to elevate their consciousness to a state where it can access more light and beneficial energies.

Being a conscious person brings you into an authentic relationship with yourself and gives you courage to dig deep within to see the truth of YOU. Minding the consciousness you keep means promoting the nobler aspects in you and minimizing the inferior parts of you. It is cultivating a working understanding of fear, monkey mind, scarcity consciousnesses, negative programming and limiting mindsets - mitigating these to put your best consciousness into the world.

Getting On the Beam

It is impossible not to think or to think of nothing. Nonetheless, thoughts have power and an effect on you and those around you. It is, therefore, elementary not to squander them, but to give them a positive direction. As thoughts shape our mental state and nature, the key challenge for anyone is to meet and overcome and master their inferior or problematic nature. This is not an easy or popular task. Who really wakes up in the morning and says: "*Today I am looking forward to engaging and conquering my inferior nature!"* And how many people do you know who brag about uprooting their undesirable traits? Instead, people run away from these. Right? However, the effort must be taken, the work must be done. Transformation takes time. And I say it again, by transforming yourself, you transform the world. By stepping into the waters of transformation one may find the work quite experiential and explorative, even liberating. One can in time, develop a comfort and preference with the new 'self' and consciousness that emerges. The following simple exercise takes only a moment and can be applied to situations where you may want to transform an unwanted personal trait or tendency.

1. *An obstacle occurs.*

2. *Realize in that moment how you are reacting, and that your reaction, if negative (emotional or behavioral) is the real enemy, or problem, not the obstacle. Be clear about this.*

3. *Shut down your impulse to react or to resort to negativity, allow pause and space for the 'light' and fresh energy to flow into the situation. Ask for it.*

4. *Express your proactive nature by replacing the impulse to react negatively with an affirmation such as: "This situation is not beyond me; there is a solution to this, and I will uncover it"; or "I will look more deeply into this situation to see what is there to discover, or what lessons it has for me." Here, you immediately diffuse the impulse to overreact or respond with negativity.*

This sample exercise in transformation is simply having a different kind of conversation with yourself and shifting and replacing knee-jerk or systemic thoughts and emotions that hinder you with beneficial ones. This requires commitment, presence of mind, self-knowledge, and repetition. With continued practice you can produce phenomenal internal shifts.

Purifying your thoughts and emotions to bring in more light and raise your energetic vibration involves being aware of the kinds of impressions you are taking into your consciousness. This is surely a two-way process, which considers your internal climate - of what is going out from you and what you are taking in and absorbing. Question and discern what you take into your consciousness. When you keep the eyes of your mind open, and when you examine what is presented to you, you are nurturing and safeguarding your psyche/consciousness. Pursuing alternative sources of information, being receptive to fresh and new ways of looking at things, and harvesting wisdom keeps you in flow. Wisdom opens more pathways and portals for light and positive energy to fill your being and your life – putting you on the beam!

Before leaving this chapter I am inspired to introduce to you a young man I recently met who is absolutely on the beam. Tall, with an amiable countenance, he is a banking officer named Juan. *During my appointment with Juan we easily got into a conversation about personal growth. Juan read a lot on that subject and wanted to share something with me about the Greek philosophy of 'stoicism' and the knowledge he was gaining from it. He told me how he chose not to react when he was caught up in a traffic delay by getting angry because it was making him late, but to see it as "Not his problem" and treating the delay as presenting him with a choice to be proactive and to find something productive to do while having to sit in his car. He said, "There is so much we should be learning and should have learned, but we are not being taught", and how he was noticing that people's attention spans were shortening. Juan firmly stated that he "Tried to get smarter every day" because he was not going to be someone who was 'complacent, stagnant or rotting' by not learning and growing.* Juan moved me with his sense of wonder and the curious and intelligent way he viewed and approached the world. I left my meeting with him with the widest smile of pride, hope and gladness for him and his generation, and grateful that I could have that encounter with him.

TOOLBOX

1. _Understand Your Relationship with Fear._

   a) First and foremost, understand that you are always in a relationship with fear - and that you control this relationship. Keep an eye out for fear and the ways it tends to show up in your inner and outer life. Make a concerted effort to know your deep and abiding fears; get to know the degree to which you react to certain situations with fear; know the mental and emotional habits you display which are spawned from fear. Monitor your fear triggers, impulses, and reactions. Be aware of how fear feels in your body. The more you know these things, the less control fear has and the easier you can transform the relationship.

   b) Understand the nature of fear – like smoke, and that it is essentially a reactive dynamic that is triggered by certain circumstances or signals. Fear is a bully. It is 'passing through' and you choose if you want it to stay or not. And for these reasons, know that fear does not belong to you. Be proactive by studying fear objectively, put it under the microscope. Keep the checklists presented in this chapter at hand and refer to these on what fear and monkey-mind look like. Seeing these for what they are diffuses their temptation and they cannot grab onto you unless you let them.

   c) Anesthetize the fear from your empowered state of awareness and control over it. Have an internal dialogue where you say: "This fear does not belong to me, I don't want it, and don't need it. It serves no purpose." You might even say: "Thank you in advance for whatever you might be trying to tell me, now you can go away." Have fun with this because humor and fear cannot occupy the same space. In another sense, fear can be a 'teacher'; allow your wisdom to discern this.

   d) Be mindful that fear is contagious. There are fearful places, fearful people, and fearful situations. Recognize and mitigate and distance yourself from these, no matter how enticing these may be.

2. _Make Friends with Your Shadow._

   Your shadow is the dark/mysterious aspect of your ego and is the Unknown part of yourself that you may not know well, if at all (Johari Window). Through honest reflection, search yourself and come to terms with any self-defeating attitudes and beliefs you have about yourself or life in general. Ask yourself questions: "What do I like about myself? Do I love and care about myself? What are the negative thoughts I have about myself? Where did I get these thoughts and beliefs? In what ways do I sabotage myself?" List the things about your personality that get you into trouble or work against you and that you feel you need to change. Keep in mind that mental and emotional habits were formed over a long time and are not easy to change or vanquish. Being aware of these habits, owning and managing them gets you halfway there.

3. _Acknowledge and Embrace Your GOOD._

   Through honest reflection, search yourself to acknowledge the wholesome attitudes and beliefs that you hold about yourself and that support you. Ask yourself: "What do I appreciate and value about myself? Why do I think and believe these things?" List the character attributes that work for you. Decide to build upon these. An important part of being happy and satisfying your heart's desire is finding your hidden treasures - your talent and gifts. You have a responsibility to endeavor to fulfill your potential, no matter what circumstances you may be experiencing.

4. _Process Your Mental, Emotional and Spiritual Life._

   At the end of the day, endeavor to make it a practice to reflect to process your day by asking yourself certain questions: Did you serve yourself and your highest good today; did you incur negative karma, or did you keep the balance; and what, if anything, can you do differently to make tomorrow a more prosperous day? Processing this way is also good for mental and emotional well-being.

5. _Refine Your Inner 'Dialogue' and Watch for 'False Scripts'._

You talk to yourself more than you talk to anyone else. We all do. Think about that. What you say to and about you in your private mind - when said often enough, comes true. Make it a practice of your personal growth to monitor your 'self-talk' - the inner conversations you have with and about yourself and the opinions you hold about you. Discern what you take in to be true about yourself from others and how you make these your own, which may be false scripts. Learn to distinguish between what people think about you and what you think about yourself. This includes your friends, family, and authority figures. Dispel negative thoughts and replace these with positive ones. I often tell myself that, 'What other people say and think about me is none of my businesses'. Find every opportunity to affirm yourself. The more you do this, the more you grow your self-esteem and confidence.

Additionally, life's challenges tempt us to struggle against something and that gets integrated into our internal dialogue, which becomes a 'dialogue of struggle' against something - be it a person, circumstance or task. This is fear-based and de-energizing. Shift the internal dialogue from centering around fighting against to escape something to a dialogue that is moving you towards something. It is the 'struggle' that energetically keeps you bound to the thing or circumstance you wish to release yourself. Keep your sights on the 'goal' rather than on the struggle no matter how compelling or overwhelming it may be.

6. _Forgive Yourself._

You are not perfect and that is not the goal. You will say, do and even think the wrong things that might even make you stop and wonder: 'What was that all about?' Forgive yourself for your foibles and shortcomings. No one beats up on 'you' more than 'you' do; so, it is prudent to keep that in check and not overdo it. It is not healthy and self-defeating to habitually feed yourself that kind of negative energy. Acknowledge what you did, why, resolve to do things better next time, forgive yourself and move on.

7. _Don't Play the Victim._

   People who habitually play the victim are unfortunate. They make themselves into toys because victims get played with. It is a notoriously self-destructive habit. Victims maintain a persecution complex. Victims feel that the world owes them something or that someone is out to get them. In their world, everybody is wrong, and they are right. Victims blame others for their own weaknesses, shortcomings, and failures. They avoid taking responsibility for their actions, choices, and mistakes. Victims are never satisfied. These behaviors are for children, not adults. Choosing to be a victim is one of the most lethal impediments to your growth and access to light. This habit is a life killer as it saps and obstructs your life force and energy. The habitual victim is essentially a fearful and insecure person who retreats into self-pity for comfort. Resist the warm and artificial safety that feeling the victim provides. Instead, affirm that you are in control and the warden of your house of dreams.

8. _Acknowledge and Redirect the Anger and Rage._

   Unmitigated anger is just as toxic as being a habitual victim, and it is a form of deep fear. Rage is excessive anger that can turn violent. While some anger is justified and can be a tool and even a strength, anger that is raw, uncontrolled, unfocused, and expressed as part of a lifestyle attitude is seriously self-harming. This kind of anger causes you to make poor decisions and choices and can injure your life. Often anger is its own reward. Realize that anger is negative energy that brings more of the same. The universe responds to habitual anger by providing circumstances that will foster more anger. Isolate the source of anger. Talk to it. Ask it questions: "What does it want.". Ask: "Where does that impulse originate, and how does it serve me?" "What is its intrinsic value to me?" Remember that the 'anger' is not YOU. You choose to take it on and make it a part of your life. Turn the anger into something else. Redirect it to a creative expression or turn it into a determination to achieve. Because anger is just another kind of energy for you to use and apply through your free will.

9. *Avoid Being Overly Cynical.*

Habitual cynicism is another form of anger, which also stems from fear, insecurity, and scarcity consciousness. Cynicism can be tempting - negativity can be entertaining. These can make you seem more interesting at times as opposed to being a boring person who does not cast entertaining negative dispersions into the social landscape. Cynicism provides a fleeting sense of pleasure and satisfaction. However, it is a voracious impulse that must be continuously fed. And while being fed, it feeds on the person indulging this mental habit. A moment of cynicism is not worth the long-term effects it cycles back to you. Every act has its return. Habitual cynicism further distances you from light and the desires of your heart that flow on the currents of positive energy. Gossip is a child of cynicism. The truth is that being a less cynical person can bring you into deeper and authentic relationships with yourself and others. People will approach you and trust and feel comfortable and safe with you. Cleansing cynicism from your consciousness purifies your psyche and opens the channels for positive energy, light, and insights to come your way.

10. *Guard the Consciousness You Keep.*

We live in an imperfect world that is always confronting us with negative situations. Therein, lies the challenge of 'mental alchemy', which one must practice each day. Be aware that approximately 75% of the information that comes to you through the media or information sources is negative. The bombardment of negativity is by design to perpetuate fear and hopelessness in life on the ground. Likewise, we are conditioned to seek what is wrong or lacking. Life on the ground is challenging, problematic and worrisome. But this does not mean that your consciousness must succumb to this and be a store-house for these impressions. You control what you take into your consciousness. Be discerning with what you 'take in' to your mind and what feeds your emotions. Channel your mind towards that which is useful and positive to nourish your consciousness, such as reading inspirational books, taking in nature and beauty, creating – which is a sacred act, having constructive conversations, etc. Guard the consciousness you keep. When you look for and feed on what is negative, that is also what you will see, magnify, and attract to you. And this, irrefutably impacts your quality of consciousness and energetic vibration.

11. *Balance Activity with Solitude.*

Being constantly surrounded by people or engrossed in activity does not necessarily enhance you or your life. In fact, this can distract and divert you from doing some of your most important work. Our minds are blasted by thousands of images, soundbites, data, and impressions a day. This is one reason why so many people are overwhelmed and exhausted – even agitated. Humans need time to process and sift through all that is coming at them through media and entertainment, people, work, emails, activities, and just plain 'busyness' - much of which is not useful and piling up. Spending time alone on a regular basis can energize and help you get clear. Visit and get to know better the inner parts of you, and what you are saying to and about yourself - hence, the nature of your thoughts. You can reflect, rest, and get organized in your mind, clean out the cobwebs, and allow insights to come through. When you turn down the noisy volume of your life, and balance activity with solitude, you can access and be guided by higher wisdom. This also gives your consciousness room to grow. Learn to value moments alone with yourself. There is nothing weird about it. Make it a priority and a regular part of your schedule. Turn off and step away from the computer and put the cell phone aside - better yet, turn that off too, for a while. These will always be there for you later. Read a book, listen to music, watch a movie, go for a walk, take a weekend trip away with 'you', think, meditate, reflect - to recharge your mental and emotional batteries. Constant motion and activity are not necessarily moving you forward or making you important. You can also get a lot done, travel further and become more interesting by just being still, quiet, and alone with yourself.

12. _Temper Technology's Dominance in Your Life._

Too much dependency on technology is counterproductive. The overindulgence in a 'digital life' generates anxiety, it blocks insights you may need, it separates you from the humanity in others and yourself, and it can keep you from being 'present' with your life. Technology does not replace the human and people skills you also need to work and live well. Give yourself some balance here. Create moments for your mind to wander free of technological devices. Strive to better understand your motivations to gravitate to and use certain technologies and social networks, and how these connect with higher aspirations you have for yourself and life. It is useful and prudent to turn away from routine technologies from time to time.

13. _Grow Through Your Problems/Be a Problem Solver._

When presented with problems that might really be trials, be mindful that you are being tested and you don't need to react every time. See the problem as an opportunity to grow and expand yourself and your horizons instead of as a nuisance or inconvenience. If you do not react when you do not need to, the seas will usually calm. This is when you can experience the extraordinary light that is trying to reach you to bring you the objects of your desire. Every problem or challenge carries within it the seeds for a solution or new direction, respectfully. Avoid becoming frozen or stuck, but rather, 'see' into the problem and beyond it. Be a ready problem solver. Be solution oriented. Being a problem solver and growing through your problems is an energy stance and dynamic that keeps you vibrating at a higher level and allowing more light and energy and possibilities to fill your life. Also know that every problem that presents itself to you does not belong to you. Discerning this is within your 'free will' and 'locus of control'.

14. *Be the Change and Desire You Seek.*

The positive changes you desire may not come easily, especially if you are working through long-held thoughts and belief patterns that are counterproductive. There is a 'best' way to obtain the things and circumstances you want.. Work with the 'expansive and generative laws' by 'being' the change and desire you want. Be the kind of person that you want to attract to you; put yourself into the kinds of situations that you want more of. Allow this new intention to be infused into your thoughts, feelings, and actions. If you want more love in your life, then be more loving, and so forth. Mentally and emotionally identify with what you want - think it, feel it.

15. *Repetition Ignites the Shift.*

Undoing mindsets and a consciousness that were outgrowths from negative thinking and feeling takes time. To name a few, these are the doubts, second-guessing, cynicisms, judgements, etc., that taint the psyche and lower your energetic vibrations. It took time and repeated programming for those old patterns to set in. Likewise, it will take repetition to transform old thought habits into nobler, healthful, and beneficial ones. Over time you become adept and automatic as you shoo away discordant thoughts and emotions as you would a pesky fly.

16. *Keep On Acknowledging and Seeking the Light.*

Contain those worrying spells that block your view and access to light. Spiritual and energetic 'light' is never far away and always within reach to work its magic in your life. Staying tuned in to the 'light' is recognizing and embracing the universal laws of mind and spirit that are always operating in your life - minute to minute, breath by breath. Conduct your life in harmony with these laws. Be joyful and in gratitude that these are there working with you; welcome and wink at the miracles that come your way. This keeps you in magnificent flow.

CHAPTER EIGHT

LIFE ON
THE GROUND

Service to others is the rent you pay for your room here on earth.
- Muhammad Ali

The World Matrix

In the movie, *The Matrix,* the machines took over and stored billions of humans in vast fields of tubular silos; humans subsisted on a 'liquid' substance fed intravenously throughout their biological lifespans in an induced comatose state. The machines incubated the humans' bodies to harvest their energy, while streaming a perpetual 'fabricated life' dream into their dormant minds, which were all hooked up into the machines' diabolical hardware. Humans were literally turned into batteries with their energy siphoned off to sustain the power and rule of the machines. The hit movie presented a gripping and unimaginable futuristic picture of life on earth. However, when one studies the mode of life on the planet today there might already be some resemblance to this scenario being played out. The *'machines'* in today's world is the collective consciousness of humankind and the primary systems that this consciousness is parenting in the world. Consciousness rules. Humankind's collective consciousness generates the social systems and institutions of commerce, economies, education, politics, government, media and religion on the planet. For centuries this collective human *'consciousness'* has been slanted towards a Newtonian/rational view of reality that has informed our way of life; and it is behind most of the serious and long-standing problems in the world,

133

as well as the imbalances in the collective human psyche. A result of this imbalance is the distraction and diversion of the vibrant *energy* needed to cultivate an elevated consciousness that can generate a world that works better for everyone in it. This is a mouthful way of saying that *we are the machines, aided and abetted by our technologies – eating ourselves alive.*

I see a bifurcated world today, whereby on the one hand it is a marvelous, abundant, and beauteous domain in which we have the free will and privilege to live and evolve as sentient beings; on the other hand, the troubled world landscape is compounded by the accelerated pace of change and uncertainty and thus, stymies us individually and collectively. The latter is the focus here of *life on the ground.* So, we get to it.

The legacy of prior generations of humans and which continues is a patchwork of a world in disarray. There is: Rampant corruption at the highest echelons of business and government which is eroding our trust in politicians and leaders; greed, which is widening the gap between those who have much and those who need; rising austerity and privatization and the loss of privacy; high and chronic homelessness, unemployment and job insecurity on a global scale; global protests which are mushrooming from people who are increasingly being squeezed and robbed of economic security, justice and basic social safety nets; rising rates of crime; human and environmental rights violations on massive scales; the reckless depletion of natural resources and endangered species, with ages old arctic glaciers now decomposing; surging militarism and dangerous stalemates among nations; factionalism and declining respect and faith in religious and educational systems and values; and a rising culture of shallowness and intolerance, with people being dumbed down and resorting to one-dimensional mindsets. Whew!

A lot and more is happening and faster and in shorter cycles, which significantly impacts how we live and work 'on the ground'. Work, being a static and dominant part of most people's lives looms large in its modern-day spoils. Corporations are now considered as 'persons' with the same rights, and they rule. The job protection guarantees and secured retirement policies that were in place a generation ago are no longer the norm or tradition in most so-called developed and civilized societies. People are routinely released from a job on a moment's notice when terminations were once required to be given at least two weeks in advance. Today a person who had spent many years on their job can walk into the office on a day and be told that same hour to empty their desk and be escorted from the building – with no cause – and this is legal! Employees are not expected to retire from the jobs they are hired into. It is now acceptable and expected for people to move through jobs in short cycles - 1-2 years and less, compared to the long-term pension-based work cycles of yesteryear. In fact, being employed at the same company for 2 years is a long time today – a tenure of 2 years or longer at the same place is not as valued as it once was, nor is it a qualifier for a next job, and it puts one at risk of losing ground and pace in the brisk job market. People are expected to move around, gather experiences and skills from various employments. We are in the age of 'zero hours' as an employment model - with people working on-call for hours at a time – often working multiple jobs to make ends meet, or just short-term and part-time jobs as a lifestyle. In fact, a 'gig' economy is firmly in place, parallel to the usual 9 to 5 full employment model. Durability is a thing of the past, with products and especially technical devices and equipment being routinely manufactured with 'built-in obsolescence'. Nowadays, copiers, and printers are light and disposable with consumers paying more for the ink than the machine. We are enticed and driven to upgrade computers, phones and software more often just to keep up with technological advances. A brand-new car loses half its value the moment it is driven off the dealer's showroom floor. Even relationships and friendships are shorter term - as people move in and exit one another's lives as if in pace with steadily advancing technologies. Rapidity and manipulation are hard-wired into the media and social communications, which promote consumerism, transience and hype for the most part; media and social communications are increasingly geared to accommodate the shortening attention spans of the general public - stoking doubt and fear over beneficial insights.

One needs only to watch the news headlines at any given time or day to witness the enduring patterns of human infidelity that seem to plague, stymie, and sap the human spirit. Taking in the 'news' headlines, which is now 'infotainment' becomes an exercise to see just how bad things are. It can be tempting to assume a 'victimized' posture and resign in apathy while facing the world today. This harkens back to the dinner conversation with the modern generation adults in Berlin where the consensus regarding the state of the world and their role in it was a *concern* but was overruled by a sense of helplessness and powerlessness in it all. However, assuming helplessness and powerlessness are not real options.

Humankind is in a *'crises of consciousness'*. This is a position that many modern-day philosophers, theologians, faith and even world leaders hold. The preponderance of 'rationalism and materialism' in the global mind and landscape foments this 'crises', which ironically, makes it hard to live as a 'conscious' being in this world. Even so, in this checkered landscape, the *consciously conscious* person has leverage!

Right Response

The world landscape reflects a *legacy* consciousness that stems from generations of civilizations influenced primarily by rationalism and materialism as opposed to universal values and I might say, virtues. The consciousness that predominates and which has shaped the world thus far is *fear-based* and reflects a scarcity consciousness. And yet, the more prudent responses when facing the world today would be *humility, curiosity, advocacy,* and *presence* rather than hopelessness. This *humility* is to know that the world today is fundamentally a creation of the collective human psyche. We generated this - this state of affairs came from us.

With *curiosity*, one needs to acquire the knowledge to understand the world better - from a higher place - to see all the pieces and relationships between these, from both objective and subjective purviews. From this vantage point one can ponder what is possible for humankind - one can see farther into the apertures the opportunities rather than the chaos, lack and danger. Delight and wonder are needed to stretch humankind. These flow from an abundance consciousness - to become open and to explore other ways of being. The right response when facing today's world would be proactive and to *advocate* for humankind - beginning with oneself.

As I have stated repeatedly, and which cannot be stated enough, universal laws regulate the lives of the individual and collective humanity. These laws are irrefutable and reflect divine order. That which applies at the micro individual level also applies at the macro humanity level. The expansive universal laws manifest according to our individual and collective energetic vibrations; and these unerringly regulate to 'evolve' realities, persons and civilizations. And here's this: *'That which reaches its furthermost extreme must naturally swing back towards a center'.* Based on this principle, the human kingdom is reaching a turning point as our collective consciousness extremes must and will swing back towards a 'new' vista. And there are signs that this is happening. The right response when facing the world today is to acknowledge this shift and be *present* in the awareness that you are a part of this 'balancing' effect.

The Pendulum Swings Towards a New Vista

The collective consciousness of humans is not yet considerably evolved, with the majority of people on the planet living outside themselves to a fault. It is an unfortunate truth that most human beings are not conscious of the essential creative power of thought and subsequently, they are unaware that negative thoughts can only produce detrimental outcomes. Destructive energies that are produced from negative thought patterns are much of the cause of the hardships, violence and problems that confront humanity. Most people pay no attention to the deeper nature of their thoughts; and this is indelibly reflected in the level of consciousness that humanity has attained at this juncture in our collective spiritual evolution.

However, there is mounting optimism that the upheavals the world is presently experiencing signal and reflect a collective initiation that is underway in this third millennium - an initiation into a leap of growth for humanity. No doubt, the cosmic pendulum is swinging from the fear-based *'thought'* extremes that have been the blueprint of the world psyche up to now towards a new vista - another mindset. Epic events are helping to spur this along. For example, The COVID virus stemmed from one infection which, in a short period of time impacted each of our lives. The pandemic shook us up and shoved our individual and collective lives out of whack. It shut us down and shut us in, forcing us into rapidly different lifestyles - tearing us away from things we long took for granted. It surfaced a myriad of hidden problems both individually and collectively. The pandemic was a monumental example of a change we were not prepared for and had no option but to adapt and alter our lives because of it. It is reported that multitudes of people emerged from the global episode more self-aware due to the forced isolation, and more appreciative of relationships, good health, and quality of life; people emerged more open to new possibilities for life on the planet; they had revised values, perspectives, and were looking for more meaning - deeper with themselves, as well as behind the green screen of 'present day reality'. Experts contend that we are in a 'new normal', whereby pandemics will come again, and again. Covid literally 'united' us. Perhaps, it left its mark, giving us collectively, a taste of what that 'unity' is like; with more such epidemics maybe we will come to like it. Going further, the sad incident of the racial killing of George Floyd sparked a global reckoning on long overdue justice and equality in our 'trusted' institutions. Technology helped to capture, expose, and tell that. The majority of those who spoke and shouted the loudest and led protests around the globe were modern generation folks. That made an impression that is still with us.

This author contends that these *developments* indicate a shift in the deep collective human consciousness which generated events to prompt more of us to evolve. Perhaps, we are indeed in the age of epic, even cataclysmic events, both hard and glorious, that will continue to stir and evolve our collective consciousness. We can bet that more 'earth and consciousness shattering' events will come. It has yet to be known that the pandemic and the global social uprising following George Floyd's death might have left super openings for new ways of doing our lives, and of understanding and approaching world problems - even new ways of thinking about ourselves. With these possibilities and the emergent consciousness championed by modern generations, this is a fabulous time to be alive.

My long connection with young adults and the 'new people' makes it clear that they are aligned with and part of the rising 'new consciousness' that is shifting humanity away from the fear-based legacy of rationalism and materialism. Adult members of those generations that follow the Boomers (Millennials, Gen Z, Alphas, etc.), for the most part come into this life with a consciousness more predisposed and attuned to universal principles and truths. They are on a different wavelength altogether. And I believe that this is by a Higher design. Fearless, organized, and independent people are bringing a new energy and intention into the world – a 'great awakening'. They are the 'balancing effect'. They are committed to fresh visions and actions needed in the world. This is the energy that is challenging injustice and a defunct status quo. My peers and I believe without a doubt, that the plague of racism and the many 'isms' that characterize humanity's time on earth will dissipate from the consciousness that modern generations are bringing into the world. With the onset of modern generations the rate of interracial and cross-cultural marriages is the highest it has ever been, with untold millions of bi-racial people being born every year and dramatically altering the human complexion of the planet. The world is acknowledging the increasing exposures of hypocrisy and corruptions through the eyes and voices of modem generation adults. This energy is behind the ideas, innovations and breakthroughs happening today, and which are meeting and addressing long-entrenched problems. This energy embraces and promotes the release of the human spirit through greater community and values for quality over quantity in the life experience. Truly, it boggles my mind to imagine what the world will look like 5-10 years from now!

Adults, 20-39 years of age are the majority populace in most nations today. In fact, the world population is the youngest that it has ever been! You are the *change*. Your generations are in the position to define and shape what comes next for life on the ground. You are the modern-day pioneers – the vanguard; you are rewriting the script – seeing what needs to be seen, righting the wrongs - making tomorrow today. Where you lead the world will follow.

A New Meaning of Work

There is a lot of work to do! The state of the world and the shifting of the pendulum requires all 'hands on deck' just as a ship captain would say. Indeed, all hands are required to keep the ship afloat when it is in danger of sinking. This analogy certainly applies today. The world ship is not doomed to sink but needs intrepid captains and crew at the helm.

The world has different needs today than it did in past generations. World wars may not be on the horizon, but inequality, corruption, devastation in earth's ecosystem, and a pandemic of 'spiritual laziness' are in our faces and meeting us head on, with a host of other new-fangled crises in the world. While we have witnessed that technology will no doubt spiral ahead and take care of itself, the world needs more responsible leaders, equity, bolder advances in science and medicine, beneficent workplaces, and a healthy, vibrant and sustained natural environment, etc. The role of the conscious person today is to realize that your life is not isolated from the general dynamics occurring in the world - which are being generated by other men and women in your own and in other countries. The conscious person plays a dual role to tend to the affairs of his and her individual life while doing their part to help steer the world ship towards a new vista. The conscious person works for him and herself and works for the world.

Work is endemic to each life – even among the wealthy; that money is there because somebody 'worked' for it. For most, working to sustain a personal living is a must unless you are rich and have the means to support yourself and those close to you for a lifetime. We work for many reasons - we work to eat and pay bills, to take care of others, we work to create something, or we work for a cause. For some, it is the work that keeps them going and is a vehicle for 'deliverance' – one way or another.

Modern generation adults are increasing their ranks in business leadership, politics and as entrepreneurs. And as the world and its governments are becoming more under corporate control, this is paramount. The complex and dynamic world can use a lot more mindful and humane leadership, and there is plenty of room for this. Bringing your best self to the leadership role and mindfulness of the connections that we all share is more vital now than ever before. The work you do for yourself and for the world requires certain skills both practical/technical - hard skills and soft skills such as interpersonal or 'people' skills. Soft skills are crucial now as work life is becoming more digitized, remote and with less and less direct physical personal contact. The reality is that eighty-five percent of anyone's effectiveness, both in the workplace and in social life, is based on their 'soft skills'. Rote technical capacity and experience account for only fifteen percent of a person's effectiveness - all the time. Still, there is something more to be added to the 'skills mix'. *'Life skills'* are now necessary in all that we do. The *'new kind of work'* that is needed will extend from you to touch the world around you and it requires that you bring your *whole* self to what you do.

Competencies Fit for Our Time

One needs cogent skills for life on the ground. Whether you apply your labor for someone else, yourself or if you are doing the work for the world, the following are the more effective and desirable competencies to have:

1. Transformational/Organic Leadership

Good leadership is indispensable. In today's world a leader needs to go beyond traditional leadership roles and be a 'transformational/organic leader' by doing the following:

a. Inspiring and shepherding ideas to address long-standing and entrenched problems in the world – to help humanity shift.

b. Being a visionary who can pave the way for new values and ways of viewing and doing things, such as building educational systems that shift people away from fear; by promoting and rewarding self-knowledge; and valuing the development and use of soft skills.

c. Building consensus and collaborations among leaders and governments to establish just systems and earth conservation.

d. Trusting more in rhythms, flows and natural timeframes, being able to have a different relationship with time and technologies. Cultivating and trusting your intuition.

e. Knowing that people are key over work systems, plans and technologies. Leading people with respect and validation to bring out their best.

d. Having a core of integrity.

Again, the woes of the world are largely the by-products of fear – a fear which is ever-present with its many forms. A leader facing the world has the right to be afraid. But fear does not have to control you. Faith and alignment with the workings of universal laws mitigates fear at the levels of the individual, and on a collective societal and civilizational scale. The transformational leader understands that when enough people in the world can transform their fear-infused psyches, the world can thrive with unimaginable light.

You as a leader can lead the world away from fear. Your leadership can impact laws and social and political ideologies that move us forward. Ultimately, you can help shift humanity's collective vibration. This can be a most meritorious leadership goal.

2. Professionalism

Professionalism is equipping yourself with the proper and required tools and knowing the protocols to function in the business environment - being organized and adopting and maintaining a respectful countenance in professional circles. Good time management is key, which is arranging your schedule to be on time and respecting other people's time. Multi-tasking is not necessarily being professional. While multi-tasking is a popular notion and practice, the idea that multi-tasking makes you more efficient is a myth. It overloads and taxes your 'mind/body' system; it increases your degree of risk to make errors. This is the case, especially with tasks having major significance and impact. Rather than attempting to do several things well at the same time, professionalism means being prepared by making more time available to do what you need to do well.

3. Teamwork

The ability to work with and through others towards the achievement of goals. Effective teamwork is a marriage of technical and practical skills with interpersonal and soft skills – even life-skills.

4. Technical Capacity

Having the ability to learn and stay up-to-date and proficient with rapidly evolving technologies, and which are relevant. The responsible use of technology.

5. Multi-cultural Competence

The ability to work effectively with and through different kinds of people in different contexts - nationally, internationally, and culturally; and putting negative and biased assumptions about others in check to work towards common goals. This is not about being 'tolerant', per se, which implies superiority over someone else, but rather, authentic acceptance, inclusion, and cooperation without compromising one's values. Accepting and agreeing are two different things. One can accept but not agree, and still work with others.

6. Service Orientation

Projecting beyond one's personal needs and agenda to see oneself as a part of the greater community and finding value and satisfaction in contributing to the common good.

7. Creativity

The ability to be creative brings value and spirit to any situation, especially in business. This is seeing the possibilities and thinking out of the box, of bringing ideas and alternatives into reality. Being creative is also taking initiative. It is trusting your ability to create.

8. Critical Thinking and Problem-Solving Skills

This is a most essential and prevalent need today - particularly in the world of work. It is the ability to analyze and see the inherent solutions to problems in a situation; and to research and introduce new and/or revised knowledge. Some problems, when left unattended can become crises. No worries. You can have at it – armed not with emotion, but with objectivity and critical thinking. Critical thinking is not the same as cynicism and criticism.

9. Decisiveness

Life is like a chessboard. We are continuously faced with the need to make decisions and choices - even more so amid today's rate of change and uncertainty. There are few and fewer 'take backs'. One must think before making a move. And those moves must be increasingly weighed and calculated. Because we are endowed with the free will to make decisions and choices, this includes taking responsibility for these. Our choices carry the weight of ours and others' well-being because every choice has consequences. This is in keeping with the Laws of Attraction and Karma – every cause has an effect. Everyone faces the positive or the negative consequences of their decisions, choices and actions, which will inevitably happen over a given period of time, even pertaining to the world of work.

When you are making critical and pivotal decisions give yourself time to *sleep on it* – practice prudence. This is also a part of being decisive as opposed to being rash. Key decisions should not be ruled by anger, lust, or negative emotions or even weariness. Allowing decisions to be guided by what is most important and from a place of strength is usually the best course. In today's climate of rapid change and uncertainty, it is best to make decisions based on what you already have in hand to work with - rather than on speculations, or 'maybes', or 'what if's'. Counting on uncertainties can de-energize you and bring you 'dis-ease'. Being decisive from a strong foundation frees up your energy for other things. And here's an open secret: Most effective decisions in business and personal life are based on intuition. Feel free to 'go there'.

10. Communication and Interpersonal Skills

Technology gets us connected but with no *real* communication most times. Social media has influenced generations of people who are connected but not really communicating and who are alienated from one other. Along with its wonders, one needs to be aware of the limitations of technology and to avoid relying on it as an 'all purpose' communicating tool. Humans need face to face, eye to eye, hand-to-hand communications and contact. Taking an interpersonal skills course or workshop is a good step. We are not born with these skills, which are learned and developed over time. Communication and interpersonal skills are more valuable than one's technical skills.

Compassion and being willing and able to give 'validation' to others where it is appropriate, needed and deserved is an important part of this. These round out your interpersonal skills and make a difference in the quality of your work and professional relationships.

11. Presence

In truth, all we really have is the present moment. Even though we by and large, live in either the past or the future. This is the push of society and programming; and it is the product of being over-externalized and over-rationalized. The meaning we search for is in the present moment. Away from the clamor of life, with solitude and reflection one can find his and her place and rightness in the world. *Presence* is *honoring the moment*, and a simple life skill and tool for personal well-being and effectiveness. There is plenty of room for 'presence' in the world of work.

12. Entrepreneurial Spirit

Introducing new ideas and concepts to the world that address specific problems and needs and building a business around these.

TOOLBOX

The list goes on. The following are additional skills and capacities that go a long way to keeping yourself spiritually and 'consciously' fit on the ground. These compliment the competencies for today's dynamic world.

1. *Self-knowledge through a commitment to reflection.*

2. *Positive attitude.* The conscious awareness of how your energy is vibrating and managing this from moment to moment.

3. *Emotional intelligence.* Monitoring and managing your emotional climate and projecting healthy and useful emotions, particularly in work situations.

4. *Continually developing and possessing marketable skills or talent.*

5. *Being goal-oriented.* Having a goal - not necessarily a plan.

6. *Being proactive as much as possible.*

7. *Maintaining a global and connectiveness perspective.* Seeing the needs out there in the world environment around you, and your contribution to the whole in all that you do. Asking the question: *"If not you, then who?"*

8. *Networking ability.*

9. *Being a lifelong learner.*

10. *A healthy and fit body.*

CHAPTER NINE

MONEY CONSCIOUSNESS

*Money, which represents the prose of life, and
which is hardly spoken of . . . without an apology,
is in its effects and laws, as beautiful as a rose.*
                                        - Ralph Waldo Emerson

Money Has Its Own Rules

There is a spiritual reality around money which prevails outside the norms
of our rational understanding. This *'reality'* undergirds our connection and
relationship to money in the forms of subtle, unspoken rules; rules that are
pertinent to anyone having anything to do with money, which is practically
all of us. Having this spiritual understanding of 'money' compliments your
intent to live more consciously.

<u>Rule One</u> – Money is for living. Living takes money. The world we inhabit
is the *world of money.* The pursuit of, the give and take, the having or 'not
having' of money colors and is fixed into our daily experiences. The dearth
or absence of money makes living from day to day untenable. People make
tremendous sacrifices for, risk their lives for, even die over money. It is
essential to everyone and everything we do. This rule does not suggest a
worship of money but recognizing and respecting the principle need for
barter that money represents. According to Michael Phillips in *The Seven
Laws of Money, "We are in the money as a fish is in the water."*
Acknowledging this fact helps us make our way in the world.

Rule Two - Everything in life that we need does not have a cost. Yet, money is a benign friend and a *tool* to access most things that do come with a tangible cost, thereby buttressing our daily lives. Here, money 'powers' our lives. Much of what we do when we are awake, and sleeping is related to money - working, shopping, traveling, visiting with friends and relatives, being creative, making plans and setting goals. Most aspects of our lives reflect some financial value or cost - from interpersonal relationships, to paying the bill to keep the lights on, to the gas that propels our cars to and from destinations, to the coffee we drink, to the use of our mobile devices, to the bed that cradles us as we sleep.

Rule Three - Money is energy. Like energy, money is generally related to action - its intrinsic nature is to have an *effect*. Whether money is being exchanged or sitting in a bank, it has a 'modus'. It is energy to be used. In saving versus hoarding, money assumes the modus of providing a needed safety net, security, and peace of mind.

Rule Four - Money is an exchange of value. Wealth and possessing things are generated through the combination of labor, energy, resources, and time. Your labor, time and energy are values that you exchange for money to fuel your life. In world societies, money is the standard by which people are valued. The way that money denotes a person's 'value' is one of the reasons why people have so many deep hang-ups about money - why relationships can be so charged where money is concerned and why people get irked and hurt more by matters that hit them in the wallet.

Rule Five - Money is a means not an end. Money belongs to itself. It is part of a flow - as electricity flows through wires. Its purpose in one's life is to be a vehicle to deliver the fulfillment of a need or a 'want'. The moment when you feel that money 'belongs' to you is when money starts to control you. It corrupts your energetic vibration. Money's energetic vibration is not the same as yours. It is a current of energy that facilitates and is not working its best when it is possessed as an end rather than as a means. This understanding allows one to reap its maximum benefits. It is wise to pursue and accumulate money for what it can do and facilitate rather than to possess and gain it for the sake of hoarding.

Rule Six - Movements of and around money will always imply a *compensatory exchange*. It stands that the receipt of money comes with the requirement that something *must* be delivered in return for it in some form, either directly or indirectly to the giver or to the universe to keep a balance. Getting something for FREE seems to be a diversion from this 'compensatory' rule, which may be why it delights and entices; but it is not. The return on something received is not always so much in dollars but in some value that is connected to the gift of money provided to the person. The universe will 'meet out' a compensation of equal value in one way or another in time. Karma can be attached to this. Keeping the promises made around money sustains its flow.

Rule Seven - Money is secondary to what you are doing. Too much focus and anxiety about money pushes it away. So, when you do what you want to do and not let money be an all-consuming concern, you increase its power, flow, and presence in your life.

Rule Eight - You have a relationship with money in the same way that you have relationships with people. Your relationship with money can be characterized by whether you have an 'abundance consciousness' or a 'scarcity/deprivation consciousness'. Our societal programming of fear influences how we feel about and relate to money and how money moves and flows in our lives. This should be diligently monitored. Adopting and sustaining an abundance and gratitude consciousness is where we want to be in relation to money.

Rule Nine - Money as energy is in infinite supply; it represents a flow of immeasurable energy to be channeled. When channeled consciously and responsibly the energy of money can flow wide and be accessed and used for what is important to you. However, this needs to be done in balance and with discernment. Too much of the energy of money can drown ambitions and goals.

Rule Ten - You are a channel for the infinite supply of the energy of money to flow in and through your life. This rule implies that one should always respect and value how money comes to him and her and how it goes out. One should keep track of his and her money - and not take money for granted. What goes with this rule is to place a respectable value on the time, energy, and labor that you expend to earn money. It is important and energizing to feel good about what you can live with in terms of what you give of yourself while earning money. _Energetically it is important to do that which is in your power to do in order to be okay with how money leaves your hands – especially in large amounts._ Being a conscious and positive conduit for the flow of _money energy_ keeps your relationship with money healthy and can support a positive flow of money to and from you.

A Financial Portrait of Modern Generations

Modern generation adults tend to value travel and experiences over accumulating things; they value relationships more and sharing experiences with friends. They value independence and creativity over routine work schedules; all of which still involves money. With their lifestyles far different from previous generations, so is their relationship with money, and how life on the ground meets them. Statistics reflect a pessimistic notion about the financial futures of modern-day adults as opposed to preceding generations. For instance, the scourge of high student loan debts limits opportunities to enter the some traditional and high-paying professions, such as the medical profession. Medical schools are turning out far less doctors. This affects us all, as doctors' offices, hospitals and medical centers are increasingly staffed predominately by physician assistants and nurse practitioners with less and less primary care physicians. Although their different values also accounts for this and similar trends, the free and egalitarian lifestyles, as well as the 'upward mobility' of modern generation adults are hampered by struggles with money across the board. Essentially, one cannot be free without money.

Home Ownership

Home ownership is the most significant purchase an individual or family can make. However, modern generations have not been accessing this type of investment to a large degree compared to previous generations. This is due not only to personal choice and financial capacity but to changing standards in the home-buying market. For example, the corporate trend of acquiring large amounts and billions of dollars of homes across the nation and world is changing the home ownership to a 'renting' market, and the cost of those rentals are getting high and higher. The standard monthly cost for living space which use to be one-fourth of a person's salary is now averaging more than half of a person's salary. As such, modern generation adults tend to live in apartments or have roommates or move in with relatives. By and large, modern generation adults tend to be community-oriented, so the new residential standards and sharing domiciles are doable and not too off-putting or foreign to their values. Still, student loan debt is a major factor holding back modern generations from home purchases and their ability to make down-payments on real estate. Inflation is rising at a faster rate than wages are being increased, generating a chasm of financial inequity - a factor also hindering home ownership.

Presently, about one-third of mortgages obtained by modern generations are government sponsored (FHA) loans, and this number is growing. These loans are accessible because of the low-down payment required and the relatively low interest rates. Many modern generation adults are savvy and well-versed in the home buying market. However, the home buying market by its nature is fidgety and periodically tends to swing back and forth from being a buyers' to a sellers' market. In recent years, it is morphing into a new landscape due to the changing financial climate and social needs and preferences, also fed by the pandemic and rising social pressures for economic justice. This is generating the re-thinking of 'real estate' regulations and procedures which may create greater avenues for home ownership for modern generation adults. However the *American Dream* remains a remote possibility in the gyrating and perpetually unpredictable market, and it cannot be counted on alone to achieve that ideal. With these limitations the vaulted flag of 'owning a home' may give way to new values – making it less of a 'thing' that a person absolutely must have. As such, there are other investment opportunities and ways to foster stronger relationships with money that modern generation adults might explore.

Savings and Retirement

Present statistics and surveys indicate that most millennial and Generation Z adults, as well as those generations that follow will not be able to save enough money for retirement during their lifetimes; this is particularly the case within the prevailing global economic system. Business market volatility hampers the income of nearly 60% of modern generation adults, with many living from paycheck to paycheck and spending more than they can save. A growing number of young adults supports their older family members and have menial nest egg management. Where values are concerned, modern generation adults tend to recognize career satisfaction as more important than just keeping a job to have money and make ends meet. Having short-term jobs and moving from job to job are motivated mostly by the need for creativity, new experiences, and personal satisfaction. The driving value is for 'quality' of life over 'quantity' and possessions. However, at the same time modern generation adults hope to retire at the age of 59 on average. The reality is that more than one-third of modern generation adults have student loans with a mean of $20,000, and 75% of them believe that the debt is unmanageable; almost 20% have withdrawn from a retirement account rather than adding to it; and 75% have no confidence that they will receive Social Security Insurance benefits (SSI) when they reach retirement age. As such, projections clearly indicate that Social Security benefits will substantially reduce or 'go away' after the currently scheduled payments expire around 2035, making SSI a tenuous and not a fully-reliable source for adequate retirement funds. With this moribund SSI scenario investing looms more as a viable money optimization option for modern generations.

Being financially prudent does not necessarily mean that one must shun and avoid money or work out a strict strategy on how to make do with less of it. An informed mind does not unilaterally see money as being bad or *"The root of all evil"*. It is people who choose to do 'bad' things with and about money. Again, back to the rules, most of what engages us every day is related to money. In today's world, *money consciousness* and *money-mindedness* are leverage. It is becoming increasingly crucial to maximize how money moves and flows in one's life and its power to facilitate the attainment of one's wants and needs.

Financial Investing - Go There!

The stock market is here to stay. This economic institution continues to be the dominant platform for managing and maximizing the obtainment and flow of money. This platform is a major force that drives national and global economies - impacting the way we live and work.

Presently, one-third of modern generation adults are investing in ethically responsible companies. Financial investing is a 'tried and true' way to maximize one's money earning potential. The returns are faster than real estate and usually in higher amounts. Many modern generation adults favor an economic model based on the private enterprise system versus a government-controlled economy. Financial investing is a wealth accumulation strategy in nations across the globe. This approach provides an opportunity for positive financial returns through the purchase of stocks and other securities in public companies. This section provides a brief and basic introduction to investing in the stock market and other venues - which, like the real estate market are ever-changing. There are some basic tenets of investing that may be useful to know. The objective is to consider this avenue for working with and through money. Here, we take a rudimentary tour of 'Wall Street'.

Stocks, Bonds and Funds - What These Are and How to Approach

Investments start with a person who wants to invest; that person hires a stockbroker agent or agency to advise him or her on how and what to invest. The agent can work with and through other persons to carry out this role which may include a fund manager or counselor or trader – all to identify the most lucrative investments on behalf of the investor. And this is putting it very simply. The basic type of investment involves purchasing shares of stock in publicly-traded companies. This provides an approach to wealth accumulation through partial ownership of a corporation. The company utilizes the funds raised through the stock sales to improve its profitability and stability. The price of the shares of stocks may appreciate, thus benefiting the shareholders. The shares of many companies' stocks pay regular dividends which can be viewed as a portion of the company's profits. These dividends often represent a significant portion of an investor's monetary return. Dividends, in most cases are paid in cash by the company to the investor; these can also be paid in stock.

Another type of investment are bonds, which can be issued by corporations or government entities. The latter usually are a form of tax-free income. Bonds provide regular income payments and are generally less risky than stocks because the principal is expected to be returned to the investor after a specified number of years.

Mutual funds are an investment vehicle which is made up of a pool of securities, such as stocks, bonds, money market instruments and similar assets. Mutual funds vary in the fees assessed for purchases and for recurring charges. 'No load' mutual funds are ones that charge no or low fees, and these tend to perform as well as funds with much higher fees. Mutual funds can either maintain the same securities over time or can have changes in their component investments. A similar investment vehicle is 'exchange traded funds' also called ETFs. An exchange traded fund is a marketable security that tracks a group of stocks, commodities, bonds, or a basket of assets like an index. ETFs generally have somewhat lower commissions associated with the initial purchase and are more fluid and flexible than mutual funds. Over time ETFs can be redeemed or sold more quickly but may be prone to extreme price changes in times of market stress.

Individual stocks and mutual funds may be considered as active investing if certain stocks change over time. On the other hand, ETFs are generally passive or non-changing. An ETF can be a grouping (index) of energy-related companies. This type of investment is passive when there is no change in the stocks. Mutual funds and ETFs can be based on a variety of demographics such as: characteristics of customers, locations of customers or companies, consumer and market trends, or companies in a particular industry grouping such as technology or pharmaceutical.

Here is how this works: *A novice investor has $15,000 to invest. She goes to her investment counselor for advice. He tells her that she can invest in a mutual fund which includes technology companies, stocks from Amazon, Google, etc. This is an active investment because the fund manager is involved in making decisions on which companies to include in the fund. If the investor chose to invest in an ETF, she would understand that the fund manager has little actual role in deciding what is included in the fund.*

As the market can be extremely volatile, shares may change price in a short period of time. Shareholders (investors) watch the market, often daily and plan strategies on when to buy or sell shares based on market fluctuations and to maximize their financial gains.

Whether active or passive, the selection and purchase of individual stocks, bonds or mutual funds is indeed the most direct involvement in the investment process. There are two basic ways to evaluate the market before investing: fundamental and technical analyses. An individual investor usually relies primarily on one of these approaches, but often makes use of the other to a greater or lesser degree. Fundamental analysis involves a detailed study of the factors influencing the financial success of a company, while technical analysis is concerned with statistical analyses and charting patterns regarding the company such as profiles of the stock prices over time. Various resources are helpful in the selection process for stocks, and bonds, etc., such as print or online investment publications, television business marketing channels, or internet investment sites.

To buy and sell stocks and other investment vehicles, it may be necessary to open a brokerage account. Brokerages vary in terms of the fees they charge. They also provide varying amounts of assistance in the selection of investments for clients as follows:

155

1. Full-Service Brokers - Personal brokers who provide various types of assistance including recommending investments as well as extensive help by providing research and other related materials.

2. Low-Cost Brokers/Advisors – Brokers who provide limited direct access to investment professionals, but good access to online and other research materials.

3. Online Investments – A venue of companies which provide an online selection of investment options based on information provided by the potential investor regarding their assets, life stage and tolerance of risk. This option is perhaps the best choice for new investors because of the low or lack of minimum account size and low fees. Low-cost brokers and advisors also have low investments fees. Full-service brokers generally charge per transaction.

Retirement Funds

While investing in stocks, bonds or commodities poses higher risk with faster turnaround and potentially higher returns, going the retirement funds route has less risk, slower turnaround, and perhaps lower returns. Most retirement funds include various mutual funds, ETFs and money market or certificate type savings accounts.

A major aspect of investment is saving for retirement. Social Security has long been a pillar for retirement income. Pensions from private and government employers had previously been the norm and relied upon for retirement security. However, most employers, especially private firms have eliminated pension plans. There have been positive developments in the form of federally created retirement programs such as the 401(k) programs, which are run by moderate to larger employers and in most cases, they match all or a portion of employees' individual contributions. *A 401(k) plan is essentially a retirement savings plan that is set up by the employer with the individual deciding at what level to enroll and contribute.*

One advantage of these plans is that the funds invested, and the gains can be deferred from taxes until withdrawn. This type of fund could be the primary retirement instrument for employees because of the 'matching feature'. If an individual has funds to invest beyond the amount that will be matched in a 401(k) plan or if other investment options in the 401(k) are too limited other types of Federal Retirement Plans or Individual IRAs could be utilized. IRAs are usually managed by financial institutions. *An IRA is a type of savings account that is designed to help you save for retirement and offers many tax advantages.* A traditional IRA uses a broader range of investment possibilities over a 401(k) plan and provides the same tax advantages. A Roth IRA features a similar but more complex tax structure than an IRA – essentially, the main different between the two is when the investor gets a tax break. A person may opt to have one or both types of IRA plans. Traditional IRAs can be transferred to a Roth IRA if taxes are paid on the funds being transferred. Also, there are mutual funds designed for people who intend to retire at specific dates. These funds take account of risk rewards scenarios that are appropriate for the length of time before retirement and can be placed in IRAs to gain tax advantages. All of this information and more on investing is worth further study and research.

Financial Futures for Modern Generations

The future is bright! Indicators are clear that we are in a new and evolving economy within nations and globally. The times are plentiful with avenues and 'assists' to optimize your relationship with the energy of money.

Emergent Alternative Investment Markets

A new breed of financial investment firms are emerging and designed to appeal to modern generation investors. This is a trend of the investment community to tap into the buying power of modern young adults. These firms have features and policies that are attractive to people who lack the significant funds to invest and have other financial barriers and limitations stemming from high student loan debt, or who are taking on new jobs or first time employment. For example, the age of automated online financial advisors or 'robo-advisors' is here, which is fostering alternative investments in the digital age - opening the investment market for people with low-cost ETFs. Low-cost platforms are surfacing which offer a wide range of investments, while affording the investor more control over their investment portfolio. These platforms, called 'motifs' are designed to be most relevant to the lifestyles of modern generations, and target them as well. Some *motif* funds include investing in businesses which modern generation adults are attracted to or involved in and may be more likely to purchase that motif, such as a community investment fund. Here, a publicly-traded real estate investment trust that is strictly geared towards developing, redeveloping, acquiring, and managing high-quality apartment communities has a two-fold benefit to younger adult investors: It provides both an easy opportunity for them to enter the investment marketplace and it is a residential option. This is one form of emergent social investing, whereby a person can invest in the same place where they reside. And because modern generation adults spend a good deal of time online, stocks in social media corporations are packaged in some of these community investment motifs. Some motifs pay high dividends.

Other examples of flexible investment models are those which help people invest who: 1. Have minimal investment dollar amounts. Here, these models provide investment guidance in easy to understand language; and 2. Have low to no-cost investment options. Here, it is made possible for people to invest their spare change, so to speak, whereby their bank accounts are monitored to automatically invest the change from their daily purchases. Some models are simply educational platforms, whereby modern investors can learn about the market, research stocks and funds, and interact with other users in an online financial investing 'community' while building virtual and real brokerage portfolios and networks. Such educational platforms teach people about investing through practice and exposes them to acquisition opportunities. These and similar examples of emergent investment models are likely influencing the trend, whereby 70% of modern generation adults plan to open an investment account or make direct investment purchases; and with just over one-third planning to change their primary traditional banking institutions and move towards financial management platforms.

Financial markets have never been this fluid and accommodating towards any populace as with modern generation adults. With the emergence of a plethora of 'user-friendly' investment platforms, involvement in investing is becoming more attractive, accessible, flexible, and prevalent. It is useful to stay aware, watchful, and informed on what is on the horizon of the changing financial landscape.

Work Life and Business Trends

Let's face it, the office and workplace have not historically been friendly, safe places where the majority of people eagerly want to get up and go to each day. The very culture of work clashes with the values of modern generations who want: Balance between quality work life and leisure - which is a growing priority; to be treated respectfully and humanely; to be creative and have more independence in their work - which is mandatory. Modern generation adults are leaving jobs in record numbers. There is growing dissatisfaction among them with the traditional 'working for the money' model. They are increasingly: Exiting the workplace outright to explore alternative ways to make a living; switching jobs for those where they are more valued and have flexibility - where they can be creative and have a better balance between work and leisure; or they are opting to be independent entrepreneurs where they can experience more freedom, quality of life and in fact, to increase their potential to 'self-actualize' as in the Maslow theorem. Modern generation adults have become quite inventive on ways to earn a good living, and on their terms. Such is the case with 'Influencer Marketing', which are emerging platforms that allow people to capture mass consumer interests to business products and services based entirely on their personal image and popularity on social networks such as Instagram, YouTube, or Facebook, etc. The keen and almost invasive interest that the 'new people' have in one another's and people's lives in general, allows for the success of this kind of marketing and there is more to come.

On the other hand, despite the exodus from traditional workplaces, the truth is that it is in the workplace where modern generations are already effecting some fundamental changes! Given the acute 'independence' and changing work ethic scenarios among modern generation adults public and mostly private business organizations have beefed up their efforts and human resources policies to attract and retain skilled millennial and Generation Z workers. This is also largely influenced by changing demographics and shifts in the labor market that are increasing business competitiveness and risk. Employers' performance and profit needs are heightened, pushing them to implement progressive strategies to retain good employees for as long as possible and to defray the time and monetary costs of recruiting and training new people; also, because they recognize and value the unique quality of employees modern generation adults represent. Businesses are re-structuring workplaces to facilitate enhanced interactions among employees, broadening incentives for innovations, offering fewer weekly hours, and allowing flexible work schedules. Start-up firms are establishing offices with open-ended workdays and office layout plans. There is the trend to have employees mostly work from home, which was spurred by the global pandemic. Firms are promoting people faster and equipping workplaces with state-of-the-art technologies to make jobs less repetitive and boring. Some corporations are helping to pay off student loans for their employees. There is evidence that these new work schedules, incentives, and friendly work life policies are indeed, boosting productivity, creativity, and collaboration because they are consistent with the values, needs and lifestyles of modern generations. Moreover, the trend towards effecting 'modern generation friendly' workplaces and business policies are having an impact on the world with the rise of corporate social responsibility (CSR) programs, and which are increasingly geared towards addressing global issues.

Making it All Blend Together

In his book, *Under Water* Ryan Dezember states *"If homeownership falls out of fashion for even a generation, there could be dire economic consequences unless renters become diligent savers and prudent investors."* Despite the challenges described earlier regarding modern generation adults' financial status, there is a reason to be enthusiastically optimistic about the prospects of their financial futures. Emergent trends in investing and retirement are making it more likely to build a nest egg. To date, more than fifty percent of modern generation adults have a retirement account; and 44% are saving 1-2% of their salaries. Relatively speaking, a good retirement nest egg is achievable by saving a small amount of money each week beginning at the age of 25 - this combined with prudent investing. And anytime to start saving is a good time!

The older a modern generation adult becomes, the more likely they will own a home - to the degree of about 50 % higher. Increased home ownership makes it likely that discretionary activities will become more affordable, such as traveling - something that modern generations highly value. Given this reality, clinical psychologists and social scientists contend that, 'young adults *should focus instead on applying their funds to fulfill their ambitions to pursue experiences. They can stop chasing paychecks, and rather collect meaningful and life enriching experiences. For example, traveling is more important than acquiring physical assets'.* The social 'experts' view advances the idea of striving for 'quality of life' over materialism, and implies that modern generations should '*Live now, don't wait'*. And they just might be preaching to the choir because these are pathways that the 'new people' are already blazing. Inherent in the 'experts' observation is that modern generation adults are the harbingers of an alternative standard of living and values – perhaps, for us all. And they are starting to demonstrate ways of making the hodgepodge of work-life necessity, leisure, and 'quality of life' in our modern age all blend together and work!

Alternative Forms of 'Barter'

The concept of money as a form of 'barter' is evolving. Economists point to a *'war on cash'*, whereby the money as barter system is assuming new forms other than hard dollars, euros, yens, and so forth. For instance, cryptocurrencies such as Bitcoin have been growing a strong presence and influence in the market over the past twenty years since their inception. The evolving forms of 'barter' fit with the purchasing habits of modern generation adults who increasingly rely on mobile devices and digital communications like no other prior generation. Similarly, according to prevailing statistics, modern young adults spend more time online than any other population segment. Subsequently, a parallel trend is emerging, whereby financial transaction systems are evolving to target and reflect the lifestyles and habits of these generations who are both avid users of digital technologies and represent a powerful consumer base. Some of the newer forms of barter include 'virtual payments' - usually connected to mobile technologies such as phones and computers, with an increasing reliance and default to the internet to transport digital currencies and transactions. The upside of this trend is that it allows more efficient tracking of the movement of money; the downside is that it generates increased openings for hacking, fraud, internet spying and the unwarranted collection of sensitive data on the public - the loss of privacy.

As we move towards cashless societies this does not change the spiritual rules of money. Money, in whatever forms it takes remains a *facilitator* or a means - not a material reality or an end unto itself. It is useful to research and know the newer forms of barter and money exchanges on the horizon, and that are taking root. Even with these new forms the *'rules of money'* are still operative. The key is to work with money and its emergent forms intelligently and from an enlightened perspective. In this way any form of money can work better for you. This brings us back to the need to keep your eye on the prize and to stay in the awareness that consciousness lies at the center of matters regarding investments, homeownership, saving, retirement and all the things that money can do to and for you. Money and barter helps you to navigate the physical reality and to be a true steward of your consciousness.

TOOLBOX

1. *Know, understand, and work within the Rules of Money.*

2. *Learn about ways to invest and maximize your money.*

3. *Monitor your consciousness around money.* Strive to maintain an abundance consciousness.

4. *Save something with every piece of income or salary you receive.* Save in the spirit of securing your financial future; and of paying yourself – energetically.

5. *Strive to have a balance between 'quality of life' and quantity.* This is an obtainable goal.

Formula 9

CLOSING SUMMARY

Knowing your 'object of desire'; reflecting to know yourself and the design of your life; tapping into and appreciating the subjective reality; operating more from an internal locus of control; honoring change; applying the tools to optimize the quality and flow of energy in your life; cultivating the relationships that are right for you and which support your journey; and aligning with the universal laws which are always there to support you – these are keys to fortifying your consciousness. Foremost also is developing and honing the wherewithal to navigate, both in spirit and on the ground.

We cannot do this life alone. I say that often and hold to that. Formula 9 implies 'work' of a compelling nature. It is completely okay and may be useful to invite a trusted 'other' to partake in your 'dive' into self-knowing, consciousness expanding and transformation. This of course, should be done at your level of comfort and trust. This is someone who can witness you, someone you can bounce your questions off on and who is invested in you as much as yourself. Doing this 'solo' is also just as rewarding.

On a personal note, it took some time for me to get my head around the facts of aviation - of how an airplane could stay up in the sky from take-off to sustained flight across long distances. Despite the aerodynamics explanations, I just knew that when I tossed something up in the air it dropped right back down. Much of what is presented here may have the same effect for some readers. And I trust that Formula 9 is germane to what modern generations need and can know and would work into their lives. Because even though flummoxed, I still got on those planes and flew around quite a lot.

I wish you all the light that you can possibly see, access and hold!

Formula 9

A SIMPLE ENERGY AWARENESS AND MANAGEMENT SPECTRUM

Being continually aware of and managing your energy is a deep process that becomes second nature over time. These questions are not cut in stone or represent any official evaluation. No one will check or judge you. The questions may sound similar, but they are not the same questions. Be honest with yourself in your responses. As you commit to raising your personal consciousness you can rely on your own sense of where you are on this spectrum. These questions are best answered after reading Chapter 4. Please answer YES or NO.

1. Are you mostly aware of the activities and sources in your daily experiences that energize you? Yes ___ No ___

2. Are there adequate things and sources in your life that energize you other than food and rest? Yes ___ No ___

3. Do you make adjustments and changes to your activities when you find that these drain you? Yes ___ No ___

4. Are you comfortable with the energy exchanges in your close relationships and/or friendships? Yes ___ No ___

5. Are you aware and comfortable with how you are giving energy to others in any kind of relationship, be it personal, casual or professional? Yes ___ No ___

6. Are you most often fully aware in the moment when you are energizing other people? Yes ___ No ___

7. Are you aware when and how you are receiving energy from others in the moment? Yes ___ No ___

8. Are the energy exchanges mostly reciprocal in your close relationships and/or friendships? Yes ___ No ___

9. Do you typically give more energy than you receive in your general activities and interactions? Yes ___ No ___

10. Are you mostly aware when you need to be energized by other people, either in personal or professional relationships? Yes ___ No ___

11. Are there people in your life who habitually drain your energy? Yes ___ No ___

12. Are you fully aware in the very moment when another person is draining your energy? Yes ___ No ___

13. Do you make any adjustments or changes in those relations with people when you realize that they drain your energy? Yes ___ No ___

14. Do you try or continue to give your energy to others beyond your capacity in the moment? Yes ___ No ___

15. Are you aware in the moment when you are draining other people's energy? Yes ___ No ___

16. Do you seek positive energy and support from others when you need it, either in personal or professional relationships? Yes ___ No ___

17. Do you talk freely with others about the quality and quantity of your energy exchanges with them? Yes ___ No ___

18. Do you have alternate personal ways to energize yourself without the involvement of others either personally or professionally? Yes ___ No ___

19. Are you energized in your work or profession? Yes ___ No ___

20. Do you make any adjustments or changes in your work and professional activities when you realize how these are draining you? Yes ___ No ___

21. When you feel drained and/or de-energized (as we all do from time to time) do you often know why and the source that is causing this? Yes ___ No ___

22. Other than relationships and work/profession, are you aware of other factors in your daily experiences that drain your energy? Yes ___ No ___

23. Are you aware of the kinds of emotions you harbor that energize and/or de-energize you personally? Yes ___ No ___

24. Are you aware of your energy levels most of the time? Yes ___ No ___

25. Is the quality and quantity of the energy you possess important and a priority to you? Yes ___ No ___

26. Are you in the habit of entertaining supportive and positive thoughts about yourself? Yes ___ No ___

27. Do you give yourself the required time and space you need alone with yourself? Yes ___ No ___

28. Are you aware when you need to spend time alone with yourself?
    Yes ___ No ___

29. Are you comfortable spending time alone with yourself?
    Yes ___ No ___

30. Do you give yourself the necessary time to spend with others?
    Yes ___ No ___

SPECTRUM EVALUATION

HIGH Awareness: Indicating a high awareness of the quality and how energy flows to and from you. It reflects effective management of your energetic health and boundaries. *20 + Yes Answers*

MODERATE Awareness: Indicating a moderate awareness of the quality and how energy flows to and from you. It reflects a need to increase your management of your energetic health and boundaries. *11-19 Yes Answers*

LOW Awareness: Indicating a low awareness of how you receive and give energy; and a need to manage your energetic health and set healthy boundaries. *5-10 Yes Answers*

NOTES

_____

_____

_____

_____

_____

_____

_____

_____

_____

_____

_____

_____

_____

_____

REFERENCES

A Theory of Human Motivation, by Abraham Maslow,1943

Conversations With God, by Neale Donald Walsch,1995

Of Human Interaction: The Johari Window, by Joseph Luft and Harry Ingham,1969

Please Understand Me – Character and Temperament Types, by David Keirsey and Marilyn Bates, 1984

Psychology and Life, by Philip Zimbardo, 1996

Quantum Physics for Beginners, by Albert Einstein, 1969, 2020

Social Learning and Clinical Psychology, by Julian Rotter,1954

The Energy of Money, by Maria Nemeth, 1998

The Indigo Children – The New People Have Arrived, by Lee Carroll and Jan Tober, 1999

You're Invited: The Art and Science of Cultivating Influencer, by Jon Levy, 1921

The Power of Now: A Guide to Spiritual Enlightenment, by Eckhart Tolle, 1997

The Seven Laws of Money, by Michael Phillips, 1974

The Tao of Physics, by Frijof Capra, 1975

The Turning Point, by Frijof Capra, 1982

Transition Now! Redefining Duality 2012 and Beyond, by Patricia Cori, Lee Carroll, and Pepper Lewis, 2010

Under Water: How Our American Dream of Homeownership Became a Nightmare, by Ryan Dezember, 2020

ABOUT THE AUTHOR

Dr. Elizabeth D. Taylor has spent her entire career advancing the learning, development, and betterment of peoples in the world as a professor and leader at universities, as a business owner, visionary personal growth leader, media producer and author. She is the Founder and President of Wisdom To Go. She was a professor at universities in the US and abroad teaching a variety of subjects in business management and organizational development. As a guest lecturer, speaker, seminar leader, executive coach and dialogue specialist, Dr. Taylor worked with corporation leaders and professionals on leadership, organizational effectiveness and transformation, diversity, women's empowerment, conflict management, human resources management, life skills, visioning and complex problem-solving. She was invited to conduct 'reconciliation' dialogues in South Africa by the SA Minister of Education at the end of apartheid.

Dr. Taylor was a nationally syndicated radio talk show host, discussing topics of the day concerning personal and spiritual growth and development needs. In her ardent research and quest for ever-expanding knowledge. Dr. Taylor engaged indigenous communities abroad focusing on personal growth and evolution, spirituality and native wisdoms in Central America, South America, Europe, Asia, Hawaii, Africa, the Caribbean and Middle East. Dr. Taylor most recently spent over five years in the Middle East as a university professor also involved with an inter-nation campaign for the education and advancement of Saudi women - acting as consultant and liaison between universities and corporations in the Kingdom of Saudi Arabia.

Dr. Taylor holds a Ph.D. from the Union Institute & University in Organizational Psychology and Leadership, and a Master of Science from University of San Francisco in Human Behavior and Organizational Development. She is a specialist in Jungian depth psychology, metaphysics and mysticism, classical theories of human growth, and behavioral sciences. She is an award-winning author with several books under her wings, including, ***Straight Up! Teens' Guide to Taking Charge of Their Lives,*** for which Dr. Taylor received the American Library Award. ***Under the Abaya*** is a colorful telling of Dr. Taylor's 5-year immersion into the Kingdom of Saudi Arabia and during its seminal period of transformation. ***Formula 9: Fortified Conscious Living for Modern Generations*** was launched in 2017 as a university textbook. From its success among college students, it is now on the scene as a commercial resource for wider audiences.

www.ingramcontent.com/pod-product-compliance
Lightning Source LLC
Chambersburg PA
CBHW030246030426
42336CB00009B/284